MW01489056

# Be Infinite

## Access Your Unimagined Potential

*For Barb –*
*To your infinite JOY*

*Sally Heidtke*

## Sally Heidtke

BALBOA.PRESS

A DIVISION OF HAY HOUSE

Copyright © 2022 Sally Heidtke.

All rights reserved. No part of this book may be used or reproduced by any means, graphic, electronic, or mechanical, including photocopying, recording, taping or by any information storage retrieval system without the written permission of the author except in the case of brief quotations embodied in critical articles and reviews.

Balboa Press books may be ordered through booksellers or by contacting:

Balboa Press
A Division of Hay House
1663 Liberty Drive
Bloomington, IN 47403
www.balboapress.com
844-682-1282

Because of the dynamic nature of the Internet, any web addresses or links contained in this book may have changed since publication and may no longer be valid. The views expressed in this work are solely those of the author and do not necessarily reflect the views of the publisher, and the publisher hereby disclaims any responsibility for them.

The author of this book does not dispense medical advice or prescribe the use of any technique as a form of treatment for physical, emotional, or medical problems without the advice of a physician, either directly or indirectly. The intent of the author is only to offer information of a general nature to help you in your quest for emotional and spiritual well-being. In the event you use any of the information in this book for yourself, which is your constitutional right, the author and the publisher assume no responsibility for your actions.

Any people depicted in stock imagery provided by Getty Images are models, and such images are being used for illustrative purposes only.
Certain stock imagery © Getty Images.

Print information available on the last page.

ISBN: 979-8-7652-3439-6 (sc)
ISBN: 979-8-7652-3440-2 (hc)
ISBN: 979-8-7652-3441-9 (e)

Library of Congress Control Number: 2022916697

Balboa Press rev. date:   01/19/2023

For my parents, with gratitude and unending love

"Life is not about finding our limitations, it's about finding our infinity."

-Herbie Hancock

# Contents

# Introduction:
# Touching Infinity

My journey exploring the concept of infinity began in a car in a parking lot. A dear colleague and friend had passed away the previous week and I was "attending" her memorial service via my phone. Still in the throes of the pandemic that changed how we did so many things, I couldn't have known how dramatically this call would change both how I think and how I live my life.

Although the COVID pandemic still raged on, Maria didn't die from COVID. She passed from cancer she didn't know she had. For many years Maria suffered from Systemic Scleroderma, a rare chronic degenerative autoimmune disease, so that's what we all assumed took her down when her health started to rapidly decline in the spring of 2021.

I'd never met Maria in person; we shared an online community exploring our intuition. Her passing rocked our group as she was a bright light with a gift for touching everyone deeply.

That's why I was sitting in my car weeping as colleagues around the world joined with her family to share memories and love for her. Remarkably, Maria had visited many of us in the days after we got the news of her death. For me, it was brief and unexpected, a poignant visit in a dream.

Despite the brevity of our time together, it became clear that Maria's circle was wide and the impact of her generous spirit was enormous. During the memorial, one person shared a message she received from Maria and it took my breath away:

"You guys, you have NO idea how *infinite* you are," Maria told her. "You can do anything. Don't wait to get up here. You can do it there! You can do it NOW!"

Infinity.

It's a magnificent word and an almost incomprehensible idea.

I've long been intrigued by the concepts of infinity and limitlessness. It blows my mind to think there is no end and that something else always awaits or unfolds.

The idea that we are infinite beings is one I have always inherently believed, but that surprising and special moment in the car brought it home for me.

Yes, I believed we are infinite. Yet I certainly didn't *feel* infinite and I wanted to. And as I listened to those words urging us "not to wait" for it, I knew I needed to understand more.

But how to begin? Normally with a question such as this I would look for a book on the subject of infinity or search online for the "Top Ten Ways to be Infinite," but these were not normal times and this was not a normal question.

So, I did what I do best. I asked my guides.

I talk with my Divine guides every day, many times each day. I am always connected to them. They are a source of great perspective and insight. They are the reason this book is sitting in your hands. I'll explain much more about my guides and how I built my relationship with them, as well as how you can build a relationship with your own, in Chapter 2.

So, when I decided I wanted to understand and to touch infinity, I naturally went to my guides. I asked them if I could touch infinity with them. They said yes.

## What You Can Expect from This Book

This book is an exploration with my guides into infinity and what it means to *be infinite* as humans in this mortal life. My guides lead the way in answering this and many other questions I asked them. We'll learn about what it *is* to be infinite. (Fair warning: it's a list that will make you stop slouching and sit taller in your chair.) Next, we explore how to get there…how to *be* infinite. Although infinity is endless, thankfully the number of steps to get there is not. There are four.

Together, we will explore why this journey matters. The best news of all is that we have guides to help us along the way.

The key element to being infinite lies in a series of events called the *Turn of Fortune*. This is a time in our childhood when our somewhat well-ordered optimistic life-view takes a nosedive. It is when there is a very real threat to our contentment (I use this term loosely here) and that threat ultimately provides our greatest opportunity to "be." This initiating event, this Turn of Fortune, may be one you don't even remember. Chances are very good that you have not yet realized the silver lining from this trauma. Processing this trauma will help you see the silver lining and this activates your capacity to be infinite. This book breaks down the incredibly complex and important Turn of Fortune and helps you identify yours.

Our Turn of Fortune "jumpstarts" our *Spiritual Milestone*. The Spiritual Milestone is that hidden pattern within us that hinders our self-love and our ability to make a spiritual leap toward enlightenment. It is our life theme and the profound context through which we experience our life. Completing the Spiritual Milestone is *the single biggest thing* we can do to get closer to infinity. It gets us halfway there. We'll also explore the disillusionment from the Turn of Fortune, the need to gather support, and the importance of trust. Together, they help us journey through our life toward infinity.

## How This Book Will Unfold

We'll start with the big picture and learn what's in our Divine design as we enter this lifetime. I call this our *Personal Framework*. We will explore the aspect of spirit and how it grows through our life experience as human beings. We will delve into the four things that keep us from being infinite. We'll also examine key concepts like guides, consciousness, and attractor fields.

Each chapter includes reflective questions to encourage you to explore and internalize the concepts. These are intended to get you out of the theoretical and into practical applications to your life.

The last few chapters of the book are devoted to your personal exploration of these topics. They'll help you identify your Spiritual

Milestone and address it in a way that serves you. This will help you recognize your hidden pattern and understand differently what has been fundamentally challenging for you in this lifetime. This insight may powerfully transform what have been barriers, blocks, or boundaries into understanding, insight, and self-love. This is the path to be infinite.

# 1

# Feeling Incomplete

Sometimes in life we opt to expand beyond the realms of what we have known. This is not an easy choice. It feels risky to open ourselves up to something that we don't understand. We question if it's the right thing to do. We fear losing something we already have. But something calls to us. There is a glimmer of light beckoning us to move forward. We are both drawn to and repelled by it. What lies ahead as a new possibility is introspection that can open our lives in unimagined ways. The choice is ours. Do not underestimate the possibilities this opening can bring.

Opening to this choice is a means to be infinite. It is a venture into infinity that comes to us when we seek it and we are blessed to receive it. While we intellectually may desire it, it is not until we surrender that we can access it.

Life is a series of experiences and lessons. One leads to another. Some lessons are crystal clear to us as they happen, like not putting your hand on a hot stove. Others have much more mystery and subtlety to them. These are *Life Lessons* that are like a well-written story with clues along the way that come together to make sense in the final chapter. This book is about those Life Lessons.

Several years ago, I found myself in a job where I was willing to compromise my own happiness by settling for a situation that brought me no joy and no growth. My long-standing needs to accomplish something that mattered and to feel a sense of belonging were unmet. For a time, I rationalized that I could make it work, but I eventually came to realize it wouldn't ever be what I needed it to be. That simple truth moved me to leave that job with new hope that I could still find what was missing in my life. With renewed intent, I moved on.

This wasn't my first attempt at finding my life purpose. I left a long-term career nine years earlier with the intent of opening myself up to what the Divine had in store for me. I intended to restart myself completely, but I got cold feet and chose to return to corporate life, rationalizing that shifting from a career in manufacturing management at a very large company to human resources management at a smaller company would feel different. It didn't. So I tried it again with a different company. Nope. Finally, I realized I had to make a bigger change. Something else was beckoning me to pivot hard toward what I needed to discover about myself. I needed to explore well beyond what I thought was possible.

In reality, I had never really given much consideration to what I thought was possible. I had been moving in a stepping-stone fashion through my career, exploring life in a relatively safe and, in hindsight, incremental way. There were ups and downs, and in general my life trajectory was steadily improving. Though it was good and at times remarkable, there was always something in the background of my life that was not quite satisfied. I occasionally got a glimpse of what might be possible, but that glimpse was fleeting. Then, as I explained in the Introduction, my friend passed away and gifted me with her message from beyond: we have no idea how infinite we are and we don't need to wait to find out.

To be infinite is to be able to stimulate and support ongoing transformation. Our transformation. Transformation to what? That depends on you. What do you aspire to do or be? Transformation is a metamorphosis that is yours to create. If you believe, as I do, that we are here to transform ourselves, there is no better place from which to do it than the unlimited state of being infinite.

I am strongly drawn to personally connect with infinity in the "here and now," on Earth, as a human being. I believe we are all infinite beings and that part of our life on Earth is to learn to live that way. It's important to be infinite not only for ourselves, but for us all. I see this as part of the Divine's plan for each of us. When you become ready, the way becomes clear.

The Divine design for us, our Personal Framework, is highly integrated and includes big issues and recurring themes that can be addressed as part of that plan. I asked my spiritual guides about what is intended for us in life. They said we are meant to:

- Experience life
- Learn lessons
- Grow knowledge
- Lift humanity up
- Love ourselves and joyfully expand as a human beings
- Co-create with all sources of the Divine
- Grow and develop the spirit
- Express our essence

This frames the broad context of what we are on Earth to do. Some of them are relatively easy to assess (if not do well), like experiencing life, learning lessons, and growing our knowledge. The others are not so easy. Lifting humanity up? That's a tall order. I do seek to joyfully expand as a human being, but am just as likely to stay firmly planted with my long-held limiting beliefs keeping me from self-love. Co-create with all sources of the Divine? Uh, no. Grow and develop my spirit? Um, how? Express my essence? What does that even mean?!

Despite our successes and strengths, we often feel incomplete at some level. We may grow weary at the prospect of dealing with life's daily challenges. We see so many aspects of life that could be different. We are challenged by our personal health (physical, emotional, mental, and spiritual), our relationships (family, personal, and work), our ambitions, and the state of our world (local and global). It can be overwhelming.

What may seem like an endless list of "things I would change if I could" actually has a Divine coherence: an order that is unseen. There is a pattern that is as unique as each one of us. It's not random. It's the exact deal that we made with the Divine before our life began. And just as *that* makes sense in a way that is not fully understood, so, too, is there a way through this complexity.

What if instead of being ever-aware of what's lacking in our lives, we become increasingly adept at living life? That's an important step toward becoming infinite. Becoming more adept helps us in all aspects of navigating a changing world. It empowers us to successfully maneuver through this deal we made with the Divine. This opens up freedom to choose to shift our life in the direction of our dreams. It's available to us and it requires new insights.

There is a unifying concept that helps make sense of our individual challenges. It's Divine. I have no unique claim on the Divine, of course. If you choose to read on, you'll see that I am simply a person who has struggled as you have. What may be different about me is that I have sought this earnestly. With enormous hope and sincerity, I asked my guides and the Divine to help me be infinite. This is not a passing fancy. It is heartfelt and urgent to me. It unfolds every day as I consciously, deliberately, and lovingly work with my spiritual guides to be infinite. I do have a unique relationship with my guides (more to come on that in Chapter 2) that gives me confidence I can move forward. It is through this relationship and my quest to explore the notion of infinity in this Earthly realm that the insights I share in this book have surfaced.

Perhaps you're contented with your life. If so, there's no need to read further. But if you are feeling even a little bit limited by your sense of incompleteness, or believe "there's just *got* to be more than this," I invite you to journey on to be infinite.

This exploration begins with the important connection to our guides, who can serve as companions and support for the journey. We will explore our spiritual nature and the Personal Framework that outlines our Divine design. We'll delve into the Turn of Fortune in our childhood that sets the stage for our critical Spiritual Milestone Life Lesson. We may or may not already recognize this Spiritual Milestone as part of our life experience, but will gain a context that helps build new awareness of what's possible regardless. We'll explore our expanding consciousness and the way attractor fields play into our behavior. We will then examine the role trust plays in the process. All of this prepares us to personally identify our four steps and find ways to address them in the spirit of the desire to be infinite. Let the journey begin.

We all have life challenges. My goal with this book is to help us understand the bigger picture of how life's adversities and difficulties fit into our individual life plan as we strive to build the best possible life we can. If it sounds like a lot, it is. We are, after all, discussing the journey to be infinite. But do not let that deter you. It's not as complicated as it may sound. Wherever you are in your life, you can make progress and you have a guide team to help you. All you need to do is ask.

## Reflective Questions to Consider

1. Consider the most significant area of your life where you feel incomplete. When did it begin? Is it getting easier or harder as life goes on?
2. What patterns do you see in your life that do not serve you?

# 2

# The Guides

Guides are Divine help. I have a team of spiritual guides (not people) that I work with every day. They help me live a better life and navigate life's bigger (and smaller) questions. This is Divine help customized for me and my journey. You, too, have a Divine team available to you.

Everything I have shared so far and everything that lies ahead in this book is a result of me asking my guides questions about how things work. My guides have been a big part of me understanding my life journey and connecting to my infinite self.

My husband and I were working in the yard one beautiful summer morning. We noticed our sweet five-year-old neighbor Anna coming into our yard toward us. She didn't see us. She was looking intently at the ground directly in front of her with a magnifying glass and a lit flashlight. "Hi Anna. What are you doing?" I asked. She looked at me, and then my husband, and said very seriously, "Looking for bad guys." She continued her search.

A few minutes later, we heard Anna's dad calling her. We looked up and so did she. She explained, "That's my dad. I can't hear him." Anna resumed her search.

For a moment, picture Anna's dad as her guide. He had something to say to her, but she chose to not listen.

Our guides are the same. They make helpful messages available to us all the time. Sometimes we hear them and listen. Sometimes we don't hear a thing. Sometimes we hear them and ignore them, like Anna. Anna didn't want to be called back home. She was on a great adventure and didn't want to do anything other than what she was doing so she ignored her dad.

We each have a guide team provided by the Divine to help us meet life's challenges. Whether you are consciously in contact with your guides or not, they have messages available to you. Often, we don't receive messages because we aren't asking for them. We must ask to be connected to our guides and to receive their messages for us. Sometimes that happens subconsciously.

My guides tell me that on average, people receive about thirty percent (range seven to one hundred percent) of the messages available to them. If you have ever reacted to a gut feeling or instinct or intuitive sense, you are likely receiving input from your guides. It is always our free will, of course, to listen and/or act on that guidance. Our guides do not interfere. In the example above, Anna opted out.

The fact that it was little Anna's dad calling to her is also poignant. Parents are a great metaphor for our guide teams. They usually have our best interests at heart, are eager to help us, and have skills well beyond our own. But where parents may fall short in any or all of the above, guides do not. Guides are not limited by the experiences, beliefs, and weaknesses that can get in the way of "good guidance" from parents.

I was first introduced to the concept of spirit guides in 2002. At the time, I was working as a manager for a large company when they began offering "voluntary separation packages" to employees to mutually meet the company's need to downsize and individuals' desires to make a change. At forty-three years old, I had worked for the company since my graduation from Michigan Technological University with a Chemical Engineering degree, so I felt like I grew up there. It was a big part of my life.

I'd married my husband several years before this "early retirement" opportunity came up, and ours was a long-distance marriage, juggling two households two hours from each other. I began to think seriously of leaving the company. I did the numbers and it looked like we'd be fine financially. The timing seemed right, and I could leave on a high note after some rocky years in my career. In fact, there was no reason *not* to leave, and yet I hesitated. I couldn't really put my finger on why.

Some friends told me about a woman who had also worked for the company but left to become a business coach. Reportedly, she had very strong intuitive skills that she wove into her work.

Intrigued, I scheduled an appointment.

During our session, I briefly explained my dilemma and asked for her response. After a moment she said, "You understand there's a zero percent chance of you staying there, right?" In that moment, I did. Then she said, "Now let's help you understand why." My guides knew it wasn't the right thing for me to stay and they told the intuitive as much. A fascinating discussion ensued as she told me about Divinely-appointed beings called spirit guides that are available to help us navigate life. She explained it's our choice to reach out to them and to use them or not, but noted they can be very helpful.

She encouraged me to consult my guides for this decision and also to develop an ongoing relationship with them. That discussion was a relatively small part of our time together, but it stuck with me.

I made some well-intended but half-hearted attempts to reach out to my guides several times in the following years, but it felt awkward. Eventually, I stopped trying and figured that this just wasn't for me.

My career outside the company I left continued on for another nine years. I worked for medium-sized companies in my hometown, where my husband and I now lived together. My interest in spirituality continued and consisted primarily of self-study.

Consider the possibility that we can have access to a Divine team of support that is on call whenever we need them. Would you pass such an opportunity up? For a long time, I did pass it up. I didn't feel it was really available to me. I had all sorts of explanations for this: perhaps I wasn't good enough. Maybe I had to achieve a certain level of piousness to earn the right to have this loving support. Thankfully, I eventually understood this was not so. Divine guidance was available to me and always has been.

Some years later, my interest rekindled and I attempted to connect to my guides again.

This time it didn't feel awkward. This time I didn't give up. This time it felt like it feels when a new relationship is developing. I began to look forward to connecting with my guides.

Since they were Divine, I started out a bit tentative and formal in how I asked my guides questions. I was intimidated by how grand they must be.

I thought about how I learned to pray as a child, which was very scripted, using words I didn't typically use.

Things really opened up in my relationship with my guides when I finally relaxed into it. Sure, they were Divine, but I realized I was too.

By this time, I was clear with myself that I really *wanted* a strong relationship with my guides. It became important to me and I concluded it must not be terribly complicated to do it. I reasoned that the Divine wants us to do it, so why make it harder than it needs to be? I began to simply talk to them in an ordinary way using my own words. Then, I would quietly wait for a knowing or a message or an impression from them. I initially had a picture in my mind of them conferencing and getting back to me later.

That's not the way it worked. They always responded immediately, so I had to learn to get in "receiving mode" right away. Basically, that means paying attention to images, words and ideas that came to mind. When something would come up, for instance a word like "trust," I would ask my guides if this was what they gave me. If it wasn't, I would ask my guides to please try again.

There are times I have asked my guides to repeat the message a dozen times. They are extremely patient. If the message *was* "trust," I would likely ask a follow-up question, like "Does this have to do with me wondering about the integrity of this person I just met?" If they responded that it was, great. Mission accomplished, message received. My guides celebrate with me when important messages are received. I get this image of them dancing and high-fiving. What can I say? My guides are a blast.

I think my guides were very happy I was finally aware of them and communicating with them. After all, it is what they are here to do, and they are a gift to us from the Divine. Not engaging them would be like registering for a wedding gift of fine china and then never using it. It just doesn't make sense. Asking for help in this life and then not using our guides, which are an answer to our spoken or unspoken prayer, also doesn't make sense. Everybody has a guide team waiting to be called up and if we're going to go to the effort of calling on them, we may as well listen to what they have to say.

Over the past eight years, I have developed my relationship with my guides. This led to my work as an intuitive and energy practitioner, where

I help people address issues that are important to them. My guides are a critical part of that work and of my life.

Having access to my guides as I embarked on my journey as an intuitive and energy practitioner and in my quest of connecting to my infinite self was foundational. It's essentially the price of admission. In this work, what comes from me is not of me. It is simply not mine. It is the Divine working directly with the human world—either with me or with the person requesting help. As an energy practitioner, I help connect the two in a specific context.

Healing happens without energy practitioners every day. As human beings, we are meant to heal, and we have amazing biology that helps that happen. We also have direct access to the Divine. We can pray. We can meditate. We can take advantage of all kinds of traditional and non-traditional healing modalities that have arisen from cultures around the world. We have many options available to us. Energy work is one of them and I joyfully work with people for their greatest and highest good.

My guides play an important role in the work I do with clients, just as they have informed the content of this book. In it, I use the terms *guides* and *team* interchangeably. I was heartened to learn that guides work together as a team: a unit of love.

A fellow energy practitioner encouraged me to explore the concept of my team in my work with her. At first, I was uncomfortable with that. I could and should do it myself! I finally took her suggestion when it simply became too much work to do myself and there was no other option.

Prior to that, I'd been reluctant to ask my guides for help. Maybe they were busy. Maybe they would think I was lazy or wasn't taking this seriously. I didn't want them to think they'd been stuck with a slacker.

It turns out, they were happy to help. Besides wanting to help, they are very good at it and have a huge capacity. And as for being stuck with me, they volunteered! So, when my colleague suggested I spend a little time getting to know my team, I was all in.

In my work career I spent twenty-five years in manufacturing: all of it was working on teams. Good teams, bad teams, productive teams, teams that failed, teams that I loved, teams that were easy to leave, teams that I cried with, and teams that I celebrated with. If there was one thing in energy work I did *not* need guidance on, it was meeting and joining up with my team! Bring it *on*!

I got to know my guide team by asking questions. *Lots* of questions. Questions like:

- How many of you are on the team?
- How many have been with me my whole life?
- How recently did the latest guide join?
- Is there a join-up when new guides join and send-off when others leave?
- Do you work in sub-teams?
- How many of you are helping me with issue X? How many with issue Y?
- Do you each have "specialties" based on your strengths?
- Are there any Archangels on the team?
- Did I know any of you from earlier this lifetime before you passed on?
- Are any of you relatives that have passed on?

And, that's just for starters. Here are some more:

- Can animals be guides?
- Were you assigned to me or did you volunteer?
- Will I know when someone joins or leaves the team?
- How much of what you are trying to tell me am I actually *getting*?
- Can you help me with issue Z?
- Am I benefiting from you fully?

You get the picture. There was something about asking such basic questions that gave me comfort and a sense of connection with them. I felt like I really knew my guides. It helped me feel comfortable going to them and asking for help and guidance on everything.

I don't only ask my guides about big things or save them for special occasions. I ask them about plenty of mundane things, like:

- Which of these two recommended doctors would be best for me now?

- How many capsules of vitamin D3 do I need today?
- Which of these similarly rated hotels is the best choice for me?

While answers to the above questions are nice, the real benefits of working with my guides concern helping others. I work on behalf of people looking to address issues that worry them or to get help reaching a goal they care about. The guides have access to all the information that has happened in the past and in the present moment and work with us "for the greatest and highest good." Without the help of my guides, the best I could offer people seeking help is my experience and opinions. And while that has some value, it pales in comparison to the infinite resources of my guide team.

I work with my guides to help people as an energy practitioner. The premise for energy work is that *everything* is energy. Issues with their energy are at the heart of most problems for which people seek help. Energy in this sense is a very broad term. You may be familiar with terms like chi, chakras, and meridians, but energy work addresses emotions and the physical systems of the body, as well. It can also help mitigate the impacts the inner and outer worlds have on you, known and unknown.

There are many energy modalities available to people seeking help. In the early days, I worked with my guides using several established energy protocols. There are many different energy modalities available and working with guides as part of the process is not unusual. Personally, I would not consider working with an energy practitioner who isn't using Divine guidance in some way.

## A New Energy Method Emerges

In December 2019, while reading a book, I began to see the skeleton of an entirely new energy modality emerging. I knew almost instantly that I would develop my own energy modality. It never occurred to me that this is something I would ever do, but it was clear to me in that moment. That began the still-developing journey of my method, *Attracting Joy*.

Since I never expected to develop an energy method, I naturally asked my guides to help. They were "all in." They have been my sounding board, my co-creators, and my re-assurers every step of the way. I work on and with the system every day alongside my guides for both my clients' benefit and my own. The Attracting Joy Method will be discussed in more detail in Chapter 13.

The COVID pandemic began in earnest a few months after I started developing Attracting Joy. My relationship with my guides took another leap forward when I started taking daily walks during the pandemic. My original goal when I began this routine was simply to get some fresh air and exercise. I enjoyed meeting neighbors during these walks and, grateful for in-person human contact, we chatted while socially distanced, despite the frigid snowy conditions.

The greatest bonus from my walks, however, was that my guides liked to go on my walks with me. Actually, they are *always* with me, but I started consciously talking and working with them during my walks. Much of the development of Attracting Joy took place during these walks. This made my walks a very sacred time for me and my guides, as well as being a built-in incentive to always make time for a daily stroll.

I had no plan or agenda for these conversations. I would either ask a question that popped up or just start listening if I sensed that they had something to say. Guides are not pushy. I would ask "Do you have something for me?" or "Is there something you're just itching to discuss?" and off we would go.

An hour later, I was home and recording what I'd learned about me, my method, and life. I love my outdoor walk time with my guides. Nothing is "off limits" and much of what is included in this book is a result of those walks.

## Where Did They Go?

I indicated my guides are always with me, and they are. But, suddenly and unexpectedly, there was a period where I had difficulty connecting to them. I contracted a moderately serious case of COVID-19 in 2020. I checked in with my guides daily and worked energetically to address the virus and my symptoms, but it became increasingly difficult to do. Despite my best efforts, I couldn't stay focused and lost my train of thought easily.

After five days, I became discouraged that I wasn't getting better and reached out to my doctor for support. Thankfully, with the intervention of a steroid, my fever ended and I felt my energy returning. By the next day I was more clear-headed. I still had constant shortness of breath that would persist for several months, but my remaining days of quarantine were much better. I was relieved and grateful.

With renewed focus and mental clarity, I began to review what happened during my weeks of infection. I tracked the percentage of access I'd had to my guides each day since I was exposed to the virus. I was accustomed to this being one hundred percent and I was shocked to learn that my ability to connect with my guides had dropped precipitously from my date of infection forward. By the time I was diagnosed, my connection to my team was only thirty-four percent; the morning I got the steroid, it was a dismal one percent.

As the steroid gave much needed physical help to my body, my ability to connect to my guides rebounded quickly.

I felt incredibly vulnerable during my infection with this disease, perhaps more so because of my decreasing connection to my guides. After the fact, my team told me that my energy was all being prioritized to fight the virus. I had no idea how much of my energy was required for my guide connection until it was limited by that energy being diverted to address the virus. Interestingly, while conversing with my guides feels easy and effortless, this experience showed me that it requires a good deal of energy to maintain a strong connection with my guides.

## A Few Last Thoughts on Guides

If there's something big coming up in my life where I need support in doing something new—like writing a book, for example—I ask if the team has what we need to make it happen. Their answer? Yes. In fact, there were ten new guides to help and they showed up a week before the idea of a book even entered my mind.

I ask my guides about things in the present moment and in the past. They are not fortunetellers reading the future. The future is subject to many variables and to the free will at that time. That said, there is much to be learned from the past and the present.

When I do this work, I invite my team in for my greatest and highest good. While working with your guides, if you ever get information that seems in *any* way vengeful, unforgiving, or "not in keeping with what I might expect from the Divine", chances are it's not your guide team you're connected to. I recommend you shut down that communication immediately, re-center, and connect again with the idea of your own greatest and highest good. This helps eliminate other "chatter" you may be receiving from less well-intended sources.

As you consider your own life experience and the prospect of connecting to your infinite self, I encourage you to develop your own relationship with your guides. They're waiting for you, and you'll be glad you did.

## Reflective Questions for you to Consider

1.  What in your personality or any other aspect of your self helps or hinders you from welcoming help from your guides?
2.  Consider an experience in your life when you may have had Divine help. How did you feel? What about it makes you think it was Divine versus simply "good luck"?

# 3

# The Impact of Significant Life Events

The dilemma of addressing some of life's biggest challenges is that in the realm of personal human experience, we simply do not have all the information to truly comprehend what holds us back. We don't have the full perspective on how a particular piece of the puzzle fits into the big picture. Understanding our underlying life theme helps get us there.

Several years ago, my father died in the hospital while recovering from heart surgery. He was eighty-three years old. His need for extensive open-heart surgery surfaced unexpectedly, but it wasn't an emergency. Our family was with him in the hospital the few days before surgery and he was in good spirits. A kind and caring hospital chaplain helped him complete the requisite "advance directive" for medical care. My dad was very firm in his expectation that if he had a stroke during the surgery or afterwards, he did not want any life-saving measures.

Outwardly, Dad was a very robust man. He loved to ride his bike and literally wore his bike out in his early eighties because he biked a few hours every day. People in town came to recognize him, always wearing a baseball cap (never a helmet) and riding v-e-r-y slowly. I marveled at his balance, being able to ride that slowly and stay upright! Biking was a very social thing for Dad. How long he rode in a given day was determined by how many people he stopped to talk to, not a predetermined distance. Because of his lifestyle, we were very surprised to learn he had such a serious heart condition.

I was confident the surgery would go well. He had the benefit of an excellent cardiac surgeon at a fine hospital, and he was otherwise in good shape. His surgery took nine hours and we left the hospital that evening assured things went well. When we arrived to see him in intensive care the next morning he was not yet awake. We learned that this can happen and it sometimes takes a few days.

Dad never really did seem to fully wake up from his surgery. The hopeful glimmers that raised our spirits were not sustained and after a few weeks in intensive care, he suffered a stroke. Once confirmed, Dad passed away minutes after the hospice arrangements were finalized.

It was so sad to lose my wonderful father but also comforting that his clear wishes were honored. I think the Divine honored his wishes, too, welcoming him minutes after the stroke was confirmed.

The next few weeks were a whirlwind of plans. We comforted each other and all those who shared our grief. We shared stories, laughs, and tears. I had moved back to my hometown thirteen years before Dad passed away and was blessed to see my parents often. There was nothing important left unsaid and I cherish my memories of my dad.

Losing a loved one is not easy. I understood the myriad steps needed in the weeks leading up to the funeral: the obituary, writing the eulogy, the funeral arrangements, and planning the visitation and reception afterwards. I expected my tears and my sudden complete loss of composure when someone expressed sympathy. I knew there would be powerful stories shared by people I loved and people I had never met. I knew it would be intensely emotional and it was.

What I did not expect was the physical pain I began experiencing in my legs a few days after Dad died. For what became two years, I struggled with chronic pain and weakness in my legs. I sought help from medical doctors, physical therapists, personal trainers, and energy workers. I felt very frustrated by this issue that limited me in so many ways.

Eventually, it got better. I came to understand that this chronic pain was in some way connected to losing my dad. My sisters and mom also experienced physical symptoms in the months following Dad's passing, although different than mine.

My dad's passing was part of my life experience in the obvious way of losing this parent who loved and supported me unconditionally. What I didn't understand was how many threads were pulled in *other* areas of my life when he died, like my physical health. I became aware of that through my leg pain and difficulty walking and eventually connected the two. I asked my guides and they said there were actually thirty impacts playing out in my life associated with the loss of my dad. Grief casts a wide net.

Grief can be an all-consuming emotion and I understood it was a process I needed to work through. I didn't expect it to happen overnight, but I did naively expect it to be its *own* thing. I did not expect or in any way anticipate that it would find its way so extensively into other areas of my life in ways I could not see or understand, such as my physical health. And if I cannot see or understand those connections, how could I expect to really address them? They were part of my much larger story.

So, why should we dive into this idea of increasing capability to be infinite? Well, because despite our best efforts, we're really not that good at resolving *some* things, like grief. We're not necessarily great at lifting humanity up, or co-creating with all sources of the Divine. We approach our Divine design from the standpoint of what we know. In the realm of what's fully possible, we really don't know much. It turns out our well-intended, hard-working, diligent human approach to things can be pretty limited, which makes our desire to be infinite a real challenge. Therefore, it's worth the effort to explore our capacity to be infinite. This exploration brings us the real lasting, loving answers we seek regarding what we are here in life to do.

We attribute so much of what causes us pain to the wrong things. My guides tell me we're correct about a third of the time. We focus on what we think we know and miss the big picture of what's really going on. There is great value in the full illumination of what challenges us. Light, not darkness, enables the full expression of our spirits in this lifetime.

## Reflective Questions to Consider

1. Notice any life events that expanded their influence on you well beyond the event itself. Do you still feel the effects of it today? In what way?
2. What do you consider to be your biggest challenge?

# 4

# What is it to "be infinite"?

Because we are infinite at our core, it is possible to be infinite in our lifetime. Do you believe you are infinite at the very essence of who you are? This is an important question to consider. We so often get wrapped up in limiting beliefs about ourselves that it is hard to imagine that we are Divinely intended to be infinite. Since the Divine wants us to be infinite, there are many ways we are supported to make that happen.

There is a Divine design that we'll look at more deeply in Chapter 5. For now, what's important to understand is that there are a lot of moving parts in making all that is Divinely intended happen. One small (yet monumental!) example of this is the many interactions and relationships we have with those we are intended to learn from and with in this lifetime. There are countless other examples of this complexity. Even when we understand this, we often cower in the face of transformation. We content ourselves with what we have become accustomed to and that which feels within reach. In contrast, to be infinite is the outcome of the Divine design.

Even when life is going well, we may sense that something is missing. We have an awareness of incompleteness that cannot seem to be filled. This dissonance is the recognition that we are not living our infinite potential. The gap between our limited experience and our unlimited possibility feeds our discontent.

What would being infinite do to fill this gap? What would it look and feel like in the human experience on Earth? Here is how my guides describe infinity:

# *Infinity*

What would it look and feel like to experience infinity as a human being? Here is how my guides describe it:

*Beauty is everywhere, even in the most deplorable expression of man's hate.*

*Peace within the heart prevails even when we are tempted toward discord.*

*Love continues to expand into all crevices of existence.*

*We feel a sense of oneness in the heart toward all people at all times.*

*Incapacities no longer matter because they were a diversion from our true self.*

*The glorious realization that we are forever loved is imbued deeply into every moment.*

*Inspiration overflows, creating new possibilities for Divine expression.*

*Forevermore, we see grace in all things and welcome their light to expand our own.*

Being infinite is not a place of rest. The influence of the heart draws us to engage more fully in that which calls to us. There is much we are called to do and even more in new areas unconsidered. Expressing our infinite self creates possibilities unimagined.

Months before I began to write this book, I made my intention to be infinite very clear to myself and to the Divine. A favorite saying (author unknown to me) is "The universe cooperates with a made up mind." I made up my mind that I wanted to experience that infinity that is a part of me in this lifetime *and in a way that I recognize.* I believe I have experienced infinity many times in my life (my guides tell me it's twenty-seven times... cool), but that I seldom realize it (yeah, my guides tell me I have never recognized being infinite when it happened).

In processing this, I've come to realize there is power in recognizing that it is *already* happening. I already feel infinite because I want to feel infinite. And perhaps by recognizing it and being grateful for it, it will likely happen even more. My guides say yes. This is my desire, and it is part of my Divine design.

During the writing of this book, my husband and I vacationed in the Ozark region of Arkansas. It was great to escape a very extended Michigan winter for more spring-like weather. I had been on a "writing roll" and it was a bit tough to leave it behind for the week. We had a lovely time. I continued my solitary walks with my guides each day (without snow!) on the lovely banks of the White River. It was on one of these walks that I gained insight (and by that, I mean listened to my guides) about Life Lessons.

When I started this deliberate journey of infinity, I first learned about the Spiritual Milestone. That understanding expanded into broader learning about Life Lessons. When I asked my guides how many Life Lessons I had, I got an answer of eighteen. When I asked how many there were for people "on average," I got sixteen. Many months later in Arkansas, my guides helped me understand that the sixteen Life Lessons are what we all come into this life with as part of our Personal Framework. It's kind of like "required classes." Once we are well along the way toward completing them during our lifetime, we have "electives" available to us. That's what those two additional lessons were for me. I have come to know them as Spiritual Lessons and they were initiated by my clear intent to be infinite. Basically, I co-created them with the Divine several months ago.

That of course, led to more questions to my guides and more inquiry into Spiritual Lessons. Do you see where this is going? It was a prime example of how it works to be infinite. I was not limited by the sixteen

Life Lessons. They were a launch pad. That launch pad was available to me and it is available to you.

Nor was I limited in making progress on the book by not being at my desk writing back in Michigan. I was learning what I needed to know while walking on the banks of that lovely river.

The Divine wants us to be infinite and we are all on the path toward that, whether we know it or not. It's like the old saying: "If you don't know where you're going, any path will get you there." I want you to know that the path you are on is to being infinite. It's part of why you're here.

Since we are all on the path to be infinite even if we don't realize it, we are also all making progress. And while time is not of the essence in this eternal journey, there are easier paths and more arduous ones you may choose to get there. Perhaps you are in a place in your life where you feel ready to proceed with more purpose toward this goal. Or, maybe you're realizing that there is undue pain or lack of joy in the way you have been going about it. There is a less circuitous route the Divine has made available to us.

We often choose to become mired in a state of inaction, which results in nothing changing and continued dissatisfaction. We may think there are insurmountable obstacles keeping us from thriving. We hold ourselves back from what can be. Even when we are reaching for what we desire, we unconsciously hold back from all that could be available to us. This same concept is expressed in a beautiful quote from the book *A Return to Love* by author Marianne Williamson:

> Our deepest fear is not that we are inadequate.
> Our deepest fear is that we are powerful beyond measure.
> It is our light, not our darkness that most frightens us.
> We ask ourselves, "Who am I to be brilliant, gorgeous, talented, fabulous?"
> Actually, who are you not to be?
> You are a child of God.
> Your playing small does not serve the world.
> There is nothing enlightened about shrinking so that other people won't feel insecure around you.
> We are all meant to shine, as children do.

We were born to make manifest the glory of God that is within us.

It is not just in some of us, it is in everyone.

And as we let our own light shine, we unconsciously give other people permission to do the same.

As we are liberated from our own fear, our presence automatically liberates others.

The Divine recognizes our desires and our fears and supports us in ways that lift us up. Allow the wave of support to carry you in the direction of Divine guidance.

When we allow ourselves the freedom to come fully into the grace we have been gifted, we begin to see ourselves in a new light. We forget our limited views and expand toward our infinite self.

Among the wealth of richness that the Divine infuses into our lives, there are essentially four aspects that mark the journey to being infinite:

- Disillusionment
- Spiritual Milestone
- Gathering Support
- Trust

We will explore each of these in the coming chapters, after introducing the concept of the spirit and its development.

## Reflective Questions to Consider

1. Which of my guides' descriptions of infinity felt the most like how you operate now? Which description seemed the most distant from your life today?
2. When you consider being infinite, how do you feel?

# 5

# The Spirit

Connecting to our infinite self has a lot to do with the spirit that activates our life. My guides tell me the spirit is that aspect of us that lives forever as our eternal self. It animates our body and departs the body upon death. It is Divine and ever–expanding. One of our life purposes is to expand our spirit through our life experiences, growing in pure consciousness, and contributing to lifting humanity up.

The winter I turned nine years old, I was sledding with my sisters and cousins at their farm. We had trudged through the barnyard and up to the area we called "the rocks." The backside of the rocks made for a nice sledding hill.

The toboggan held seven of us, and I decided it would be fun to stand up at the back as we pushed off. Bad idea. After the first bump I flew off, caught my lower leg under the sled, and rolled off into the deeper snow. The toboggan and everyone else in it joyfully continued down the hill. I couldn't get up. They were having so much fun, they didn't notice I was struggling and I couldn't get their attention. So I crawled in the snow, crying with pain with what I learned later that day was a fractured leg. I crawled about seventy yards until my uncle saw me from the farmhouse, came running, and carried me in. After a trip to the ER, a cast, and some crutches, I was all set.

When I went to school that Monday, I got all the sympathy I was looking for from my teacher and classmates. Our third grade classroom sat next to the fourth-grade classroom in an old, small, two-room schoolhouse.

It didn't have a cafeteria, so every day at lunch we walked about two hundred yards to the "new school" that housed the higher grades. My teacher decided it wasn't a good idea for me to make the trip with my crutches in the snow, so I was to stay in my classroom while everyone else went to lunch. Alone. Did I mention I was nine years old?

I remember not being consulted about this decision and being surprised by it. I cannot imagine that same decision being made today, but this was 1968 and I was a good girl, so they probably thought it was fine. Yet as the middle child in a family of four daughters, I don't think I was ever really unwillingly alone before this.

Once the rest of the class bundled up and left for the cafeteria, I was alone. At first, I was excited. There was a chalkboard and chalk! I busied myself writing and drawing and erasing. I liked erasing as much as I liked writing on the chalkboard. That lasted about ten minutes. I hobbled around the classroom, checking everything out. That lasted another ten minutes. I sat down at my desk and began to hear the sounds of the old schoolhouse. What was that creaking? What was that sound coming from the fourth grade room? I began to get scared and there was no one to distract me from my fear. I didn't leave my seat until they returned from the cafeteria. I was so relieved to see my classmates. I did not like being left alone with my thoughts and couldn't wait for my leg to heal so I could join everyone at lunch and recess.

In the context of spirit, my nine-year-old self was using what I knew of life, which wasn't much, to make sense out of this strange situation of being alone in the quiet of a building that was not intended for that. I was in "discernment" mode. This is the first state of spiritual development.

Wayne Dyer wrote, "we are spiritual beings having a human experience, not human beings having a spiritual experience." He's not the only one to have noted that fact. I believe spirits have a human experience in order to grow and develop in support of the ever-expanding "all that is."

How do we measure spiritual development? My guides tell me there are five levels of spiritual growth and development that our human experience is intended to support:

Level 1: Discernment
Level 2: Love

Level 3: Joy
Level 4: Peace
Level 5: Enlightenment

This spiritual development is a journey of many lifetimes. Within a lifetime, each individual on average spends just a smidge under one hundred percent of their life at the discernment level. In the context of spiritual growth, discernment is ego's motivation to deny love and faith. It's what caused nine-year-old me to be fearful despite being completely safe in that old schoolhouse. It's like a constant assessment of individual safety, love, and faith as we go through life. It happens without us actually thinking about it most of the time.

What gets us past the spiritual level of discernment? Surrendering our belief in separateness. We spend much of our human life in a state of seeing ourselves as separate from others and evaluating or discerning life through that lens. When we give up that lens and fundamentally understand the oneness of which we have always been a part, the spirit level shifts into love. This shift is very important and overcomes the pattern of judgment that has weighed so heavily on our experience.

We can, of course, experience love on the human level while in discernment, but the spiritual development level of love is on another plane. My guides tell me one hundred percent of us will experience this level of love, but that nearly everyone will only experience it within a few days or months of our human death as the ego's hold wanes. With the global population of approximately 7.8 billion people, my guides tell me about seven thousand eight hundred people have experienced this level of spiritual development of love during this life *without being near the time of their death.* Said another way, they have reached the spiritual level of love with plenty of time to still enjoy and benefit from it in this lifetime.

Beyond the level of love and those seven thousand eight hundred people, the level of joy includes about six thousand of those people, peace about five thousand, and enlightenment just ten people. This shows that once you escape the strong pull of discernment and move into love, the other higher levels of joy and peace come more readily. Where does "being infinite" land on this scale? My guides tell me it is attained when we reach the spiritual development level of love.

How do we move beyond the spiritual development level of love? The spiritual development level of joy is attained by "being joyful". The spiritual development level of peace comes through "being willing".

What about enlightenment then? We attain the spiritual development level of enlightenment by "being whole". Enlightenment is a state of oneness that joins fully and completely with *all sources of the Divine*. This oneness continues to build and expand forever. At a level of enlightenment, you can rest easy in your understanding that all sources of the Divine are there with you and will continue to expand alongside you.

Our spiritual goal on earth is to overcome the efforts of the ego to keep us separate and to surrender into oneness. Let's learn more about how that can happen.

## Personal Framework

Spiritual growth happens through our Personal Framework. Each of us is born into this world with an array of events and experiences that influence our life. These events and experiences are all supportive of this journey and many pose significant challenges that are ours to overcome. This Personal Framework is meant to be fully experienced by us in our lifetime.

In fact, the universe makes sure those situations arise to provide us with opportunities to fulfill our journey. There's no point in getting sloppy with our lessons or doing the minimum to get by, because we will only receive yet another opportunity to learn. If we miss one or think we "got it" but didn't, the universe keeps providing chances for us to experience it.

My husband and I met when I was age thirty-two and he was thirty-six. I had several opportunities over a seven-year period to meet him. For instance, I had an auto accident and rolled my car during a winter storm. I was fine, but the car was significantly damaged. I called my dad, who managed a car dealership a few hundred miles away, and he neatly and quickly arranged for me to buy a new car and sell the old one. No muss, no fuss. I didn't even need to be there when the buyer picked up the wrecked car.

Years later, I learned that the buyer of my wrecked car was my now-husband's dad and that my now-husband accompanied him to pick it up and tow it home. I could have met him when I wrecked that car. When we finally met, his mom was still driving that rebuilt car—and she actually gave me the cassette that was in the tape deck when I crashed it.

While I didn't pick up on the universe's matchmaking opportunity with the car, I also missed at least two other chances in the ensuing years before I finally met my husband at a Christmas party. Although I tend to be the extrovert, he approached me, and we have been together ever since. I really feel like the universe didn't give up on me meeting him, and I am grateful for second (and third and fourth) chances!

The human experience has a way of emphasizing physicality and the journey of the physical body. That is important, but also significant is what happens to the spirit while in the body. Our spirit is here to expand and to grow and it grows over many lifetimes. This is a Divine aspiration to grow and develop and increasingly contribute to "all that is." It is an eternal endeavor.

The Personal Framework is the broad action plan for our life. It's like the frame that defines the piece of artwork that we paint with our life experiences. There are several components of the Personal Framework. When it comes to being infinite, though, we will narrow our focus to only a few for the purposes of this book.

While the Personal Framework is largely determined before we are born (my guides tell me it's about sixty percent), we have opportunities within our life to expand it. If the Personal Framework is the picture frame, as we experience our lives, we not only paint the picture within the frame, but we may also build upon the frame by adding molding, changing the finish, or be-dazzling it! This is co-creation in the "here and now" and considers where we are in our life experiences. For instance, my journey into being infinite is an example of "enhancing my frame" and co-creating the next area of learning and exploration in my life. For you, this would be a product of your experience, desires, and passions. My guides tell me only about two percent of us take advantage of this co-creation opportunity, which becomes available to us after our Spiritual Milestone, or life theme, is completed.

In order of impact, here is what my guides tell me is in our Personal Framework before we are conceived:

## Eternal Stimulus

The "eternal stimulus" is common to every lifetime we experience. It prods us to evolve and transform. The eternal stimulus is the Divine drive that spurs us into action as we take form as a human being. It is an integral part of our human experience. There are several parts to the eternal stimulus and all of them can grow during our lifetime. Some examples of eternal stimulus include the essence, spirit, and consciousness, and each is discussed in more detail in coming chapters.

## Divine Design

When the Divine considers us for another lifetime, it is done with great care and deliberation. There is a purpose for such a miracle as this. This purpose is known to our spirit and we have collaborated with the Divine to co-create it with the intent of transformation.

There are aspects of this that are for the world's benefit. There are aspects that matter to people we will never know. The ripple of each Divine design extends well beyond our mortal capacity to understand it. Although this design is far-reaching, it is also very personal and focused. The intent of this design is to manifest the opportunities we need to propel ourselves into uncomfortable spiritual growth with the promise of Divine blessings. As a spirit, we enter this eagerly and with an open heart.

The Divine design is directional, a vector of sorts that points us on the path of manifestation to allow our story to unfold so that our part of the intricate universal web is made ready.

The wisdom of this design exceeds our mortal comprehension and provides each of us with our pathway to be infinite. We each have it within us to achieve infinity within our Divine design in this lifetime. My guides tell me that in a world population of about 7.8 billion people, about eighty people will become infinite through their Divine design.

## Life Lessons

Life Lessons are part of our Personal Framework. They are experiences intended to challenge us. From them, we will gain the skills and experience to move forward in our human life and spiritual development. Although we have thousands of lessons during our human experience, the Personal Framework focus is on only sixteen of them. These sixteen *Life Lessons* are very special types of lessons. They affect us on *all* levels: spiritually, bodily, cognitively, emotionally, and consciously. They are lessons that touch us at the level of our essence as well as help us grow as a human and a spirit. Among the sixteen Life Lessons, there is *one* that is essential to being infinite: the Spiritual Milestone. It is so pivotal we will cover that separately in Chapter 7.

## Turn of Fortune

People often decry the difficulty of developing through trauma and sorrow. We would love to script our lives in a way that offers fun and easy learning to propel us beautifully toward our view of success. If only we knew enough and were developed enough, perhaps this model might work. At this stage, we most often learn through challenge, however. We are living our lives to do precisely that: to grow and develop spiritually such that we co-create with the Divine to transform as a human on earth and as a spiritual being. We have co-created this uneasy path because there's something for us to gain from it.

The Turn of Fortune is the initiation of your spirit's growth spurt on Earth. It activates the chain of events that launches the underlying theme in your life, your Spiritual Milestone. It takes a lot to jar your spirit-connected self to move from the safety of the kiddie pool to the deep end. The Turn of Fortune is basically when we're thrown in the deep end before we know how to swim. It's "sink or swim" time and our human instincts kick in to get our head back above water. We somehow make it to the edge of the pool, but are shaken. And life is never quite the same.

We will explore the Turn of Fortune more deeply in Chapter 6.

While there are many more aspects to the Personal Framework, the four discussed above are the ones that most affect our ability to be infinite. This Personal Framework is with us throughout our lives and, as we experience life, we occupy more and more of the framework. Even before we begin life outside the womb, we are aware of things through our mother's physical and emotional experience. Once born and living life as a very dependent infant, our family dynamics, culture and societal norms bombard our senses. The path toward independence and separate individuality literally takes baby steps as we learn to walk and talk as a toddler and continues as we grow through childhood, adolescence, and into adulthood, making choices about how we live our life as we go. As we do so, the possibilities of our framework become increasingly meaningful to us.

We all have the opportunity to experience *all* possibilities of our framework and to grow as a person, as a member of the human race, and as a spirit. Free will is central to life on Earth, and how we engage with our framework, which is the picture we paint within it, is largely dictated by the choices we make along the way.

## Spiritual Consciousness in the Human Experience

Consider that we are a spirit about to make our way into the human realm again. We have our Personal Framework that we co-created with the Divine. The spirit joins the physical body, and when the baby is born and begins experiencing the world, it is essentially about ninety-nine percent spiritual consciousness and one percent human consciousness. Over time, the human being experiences more and more of the world, including challenging Life Lessons that are part of their path. As this happens, the percent of spiritual consciousness declines significantly as the human being identifies more and more with the world around it and less and less with the Divine.

This dynamic with the ebbing of spiritual consciousness and the emergence of human consciousness follows a pattern. This pattern is marked by a phenomenon called the Turn of Fortune, which is a series of events happening over a short period of time that jumpstarts us getting our urgent life purpose underway. This typically happens at about age six, but could range from age zero to age ten.

The unfolding of this pattern is part of the expectation of the "spirit having a human experience." We'll look at this in some detail next in Figure 1 (page 32) where we will explore what is happening to the spiritual consciousness of the human being using a graph. Spiritual consciousness is represented on the vertical axis and starts at ninety-nine percent spiritual consciousness (and therefore one percent human consciousness) when the baby is born. Said another way, the baby is much more aware of the spirit connection than it is the human connection at birth. Age is represented on the horizontal axis. The percent of spiritual consciousness begins to drop slowly as we experience life after we are born. It *plummets* after the

Turn of Fortune to about fifty-seven percent spiritual consciousness. After that very significant event, life continues on and the percent of spiritual consciousness continues to decline as we encounter additional challenges. According to my guides, on average, this decline levels off at about fifteen percent spiritual consciousness (range between one and thirty percent). When that happens, we usually stay at that balance of percent of spiritual/ human consciousness for some period that lasts for most of our life unless we address it via the Spiritual Milestone.

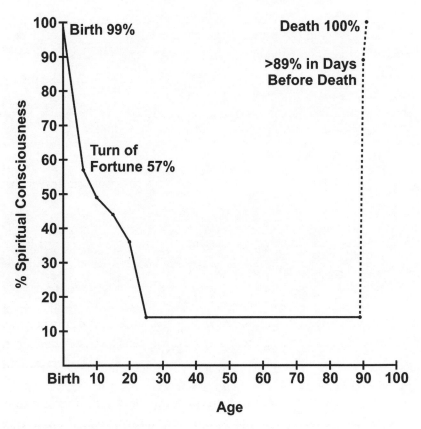

Figure 1. Spiritual Consciousness over Lifetime

In that case, sometime within the period of a few months before death, the amount of spiritual consciousness rebounds to above eighty-nine percent as the spirit prepares to leave the body. This is consistent with the phenomenon described earlier in this chapter regarding the spirit's discernment level shifting to love in the last few months to the last few days of life. This is by far the most common scenario.

I think of this process as a "U curve". The shape of the curve represents our human experience in terms of the amount of spiritual consciousness. Each of our individual U curves is as unique to us as our lifetime experiences, but all share the similarities described above.

According to my guides, regardless of how low our spiritual consciousness value is, when we are ready to pass on, it rebounds to at least what it was when we were born. If your Spiritual Milestone has been completed (more on that in Chapter 7), the amount of spiritual growth will be *higher* than what we came in with when we pass away, which is desired.

I had the privilege of being at the bedside of my beloved brother-in-law when he passed away at age sixty-three from early onset Alzheimer's disease. He was lovingly cared for in their home by my sister for the duration of his seven-year Alzheimer's journey. The path was long and the ending was heartbreaking. He was in a nursing home for only a few weeks when his hospice care began. A few days later he had a cardiac event that ended his life the next day.

During his last day on earth, loving goodbyes were tearfully shared with him. He remained expressionless and lingered on. I will never forget when his time came to leave this Earth. He bent at the waist and lifted his head and torso from the bed as if being pulled by a string. His eyes grew wide and bright, and he had a look of ineffable joy. It was only a moment, and then his body gently laid back and his spirit was gone. I believe what I witnessed was his spiritual consciousness raising in preparation for going back home in spirit. It was a beautiful transition. May he rest in peace.

May we all be spiritually conscious of this joy during our own eventual transition. The completion of our Spiritual Milestone during our lifetime prepares us for this moment well before the Divine timing of our passing.

## Reflective Questions to Consider

1. How do you feel about the idea of uncomfortable spiritual growth as the path to Divine blessing?
2. How is your free will being expressed in your life?

# 6

# The Turn of Fortune

Within several weeks of committing to exploring infinity and personally becoming more infinite, I was doing energy work on myself, and I realized again that much of what I was working on in my spiritual explorations as an adult originated in my childhood at age three. On one level, I was not surprised. This is not because I have excellent memories from that time: I have no conscious memories of this time at all. Over the years of doing energy work, my three-year-old self has come up an astonishing number of times. I have worked on it extensively, yet it keeps rising to the surface.

When I was three years old, my mom gave birth to my twin sisters. We went from being a family of four to a family of six. I went from being the baby to being a middle child. This was a major life change, but by far the most impactful experience was that my mom almost died. My mom and her doctor did not realize she was carrying twins, even after the first seven-pound fourteen-ounce baby girl was born. The second baby girl (at six pounds thirteen ounces) followed two hours later. Surprise!

Mom felt well after the delivery and during her first few days home. She did not know she was hemorrhaging internally with blood that was unable to release due to a mucus plug. It was the middle of the night when that broke free and she lost consciousness on the floor of the bathroom, bleeding profusely.

Mom was found by my dad and we all witnessed the melee as she was rushed to the hospital for treatment and seven blood transfusions. Her situation was critical. My aunt, who was a nurse's aide, sat at her bedside and could see Mom was slipping away.

Mom describes what happened to her next as a classic near-death experience: going down a very loving tunnel toward an inexplicably beautiful light. She wanted nothing more than to continue that journey. She recalls eventually hearing her sister loudly insisting she come back. Mom didn't want to come back because what she was experiencing was so indescribably lovely. It wasn't until she remembered her young family that she reluctantly turned back away from the light.

Thankfully, Mom recovered fully. She is a wonderful mother to her four daughters and the center of our large family. I remember first hearing this story about my mom's experience in my mid-twenties and I was shocked to think I might have grown up without my amazing mother. To this day Mom has no fear of death given her glimpse of the Divine promise.

While this miracle was a gift to our family, my experience of life as a three-year-old changed dramatically during that time. My older sister and I were there as mom lay unconscious in a frightening, bloody scene another aunt described as a "war zone." My three sisters and I were farmed out to different family members while my mom recovered. And life changed with two new babies in the house. It was a lot for everyone to cope with.

So, I wasn't surprised that though I'd dedicated significant time to processing it, age three showed up for me once again.

This time around, in the spirit of infinity, I asked my guides if there was something more I could learn about my experiences at age three. I asked, "Is there something I am missing?" They said yes.

The Turn of Fortune is a very significant phenomenon that happens when we are very young and impacts us throughout most of our lifetime. Mine happened a bit earlier than average. According to my guides, the average age a child experiences their Turn of Fortune is age six (range is between ages zero and ten). The Turn of Fortune is at once a threat to our (childhood) contentment and an opportunity to *be* as a human. I use the term contentment here loosely. It is not to say that everything was ideal before the Turn of Fortune, but rather that the Turn of Fortune literally changes the game for us. It is an important part of our Personal Framework and a very intentional part of our life journey. It is not to be feared or ignored. Instead, it is ours to work through on the way to being infinite.

The Turn of Fortune is a very complex series of events and dynamics that happens in a few short weeks. It is marked by a misfortune of some sort that impacts us deeply. For me, that misfortune was witnessing my mom lying in a pool of blood unconscious. While I was young enough to not have any conscious memories of this, I imagine how terrifying that must have been for my dad and us girls! We were each vulnerable to this situation in our own way. For my twenty-seven-year-old dad, it was panic and a rush to save his wife. For my five-year-old sister and me, it was our Turn of Fortune's misfortune.

As we unpack the complex Turn of Fortune, there are three steps:

- Step 1: Vulnerability
- Step 2: Misfortune
- Step 3: Loss of Support

## Step 1: Vulnerability

As young children, we are subject to many influences, positive and negative. When a negative situation wounds us deeply, it results in a vulnerability that we may carry with us for a long time. The Turn of Fortune is actually initiated through a specific vulnerability that is experienced about a year before the Turn of Fortune's misfortune.

For me, this vulnerability was anguish at age two. According to my guides and family lore, I understand it was connected to my parents needing to leave us for a period of a few weeks to tend to a health concern. Even though I was lovingly cared for by relatives at the time, my two-year-old self was afraid they would not come back. While anguish was my vulnerability, my guides tell me there are seven vulnerabilities that may come in to play associated with the Turn of Fortune. They are:

- Minimized
- Criticized
- Anguish
- Isolated

- Anxious
- Longing
- Conflicted

This vulnerability sets the stage for the eventual Turn of Fortune's misfortune.

## Step 2: Misfortune

The Turn of Fortune's misfortune is an event, experience, or situation that affects us deeply in a negative way in our childhood. It creates in a child an *awareness of incapacity* or a realization we are not enough. This is a turning point of the spirit, consciousness, and mortal self. For me at age three, I felt anguished and lost as I considered losing my mom. This is when the ego gets a foothold and steps in with harmful thoughts reinforcing the vulnerability and the incapacity. My guides tell me the ego also initiates self-criticism in the vulnerable child at this point. This leads to a palpable sense of disillusionment in the life journey that is the first of the four steps to being infinite.

We enter each lifetime with optimism and faith that we can overcome the difficulties that are a given on Earth. We see ourselves as supported and here to do important work. This purpose is part of our Personal Framework and important to the world. This is why addressing disillusionment is so important to being infinite.

The disillusionment we experience with our Turn of Fortune is rooted in anger and that anger may take two different forms. For about forty percent of us, that form is heartbreak. It is easy to see how disillusionment can result in heartbreak. The second form is fearful activities, which sixty percent of us experience. Fearful activities can include:

- Act compulsively
- Hinder thinking
- Unsafe beliefs
- Control love
- Obstruct connection
- Suppress faith

My guides tell me that during my Turn of Fortune's misfortune and its disillusionment, I turned to the anger expressed as a fearful activity of acting compulsively, which has shown up throughout my life with my eating habits.

This disillusionment, which is the first of many we experience in life, has significant influence on the child and what they believe is possible for them. That is why it is the first of the four steps to being infinite. As with all the steps to being infinite, recognizing it is the first step to resolving it, which can be done through many ways, such as prayer, meditation, and energy work.

## Step 3: Loss of Support

In the Turn of Fortune, the vulnerability and misfortune essentially turn a child's world upside down. Together they account for forty percent of the Turn of Fortune's impact. The loss of support that the child feels during the essential instant, which follows a few days later, has an even greater effect. The *essential instant* is a time when the child feels a crucial loss of the promise of being kept safe and supported by a very critical personal relationship. This is most often a parent (seventy percent), a sibling (twenty-eight percent), or someone else (two percent). For me, this was my relationship with my mom, but not during the time she lay unconscious at home—it was four days later. I was staying with relatives and likely re-living the original vulnerability of age two, when relatives cared for us. This essential instant is the time when the child begins to make errors in discernment and shifts out of spiritual harmony. In keeping with those errors, it causes their sense of love to be disturbed and increases self-doubt. With that, the ego doubles down.

This triggers the initiation of the Spiritual Milestone, which is the second of the four steps to becoming infinite. There will be more on the Spiritual Milestone in Chapter 7. In the scope of the Turn of Fortune, the Spiritual Milestone initiates our urgent sense of purpose in this lifetime. Goodbye carefree childhood, things are getting serious now.

The Turn of Fortune then moves to a denial of a belief. For me, the belief denied was "I open myself to love and joy." It's difficult to think that at the tender age of three I was closing myself to love and joy in any way. This was followed by a *blocked heart*. This is not a physical heart block, but an emotional one that results in certain characteristics that stay with us well beyond the event and may show up in times of great difficulty. These characteristics are a shield of sorts and could include:

- Back Away
- Resist
- Think Twice
- Cut Things Off
- Cover Up
- Keep Mum

My shield is to resist and I believe is part of my ongoing need to try to control things in my life. That seems like a big idea for a three-year-old, but I can see how that could come to a little girl who is living apart from her mom and is afraid she has lost her.

Once the heart is blocked, joy breaks down. Lack of joy leads to disappointment, an attack on your wholeness by the ego, a loss of confidence, and for about twenty percent of us, an agreement of limitation in our life.

This Turn of Fortune all happens over the course of a few weeks when we are small children. It's a lot for a child to take in. It usually takes a lifetime to overcome.

I do not have any memories of my Turn of Fortune, but family members and my guides have filled in the blanks. About a third of us will either remember our Turn of Fortune or re-construct it like I did. If you are one of the majority of us that doesn't know your Turn of Fortune, you may still have insight into it. How? We re-experience a similar flow of events at different times in our lives under difference circumstances. My guides say this happens on average four times in a lifetime. That was my experience. Often this re-experience happens much later in our life when we are much more likely to remember directly how it unfolded.

Your Turn of Fortune may be more or less dramatic than mine. The Turn of Fortune's objective is simply to jumpstart your life purpose. It is done according to the Personal Framework and will be pivotal no matter how much trauma or drama is involved.

# The Turn of Fortune Process

*VULNERABILITY* precedes a

*MISFORTUNE* that creates an

*AWARENESS OF INCAPACITY.*

*EGO INSTILLS HARM AND SELF-CRITICISM* which leads to

a *SENSE OF DISILLUSIONMENT* in the life journey.

At this critical time, *LOSS OF SAFETY & SUPPORT
FROM CRITICAL RELATIONSHIP* causes *LOVE*
to be *DISTURBED* and *DOUBT* to elevate.

This is compounded by another *ATTACK FROM THE EGO*,

triggering the *SPIRITUAL MILESTONE*.

This initiates the *URGENT SENSE OF
PURPOSE* through this difficulty and

a key *BELIEF IS DENIED*,

the *HEART IS BLOCKED*,

a *SHIELD* is put up,

and *JOY BREAKS DOWN*.

You *DECLARE YOUR DISAPPOINTMENT*,

the *EGO ATTACKS YOUR WHOLENESS* and

*CONFIDENCE* is lost as

you *AGREE TO A LIMITING BELIEF* .

...and it all happens in less than two weeks when you're just a kid.

Many people I work with have very few childhood memories. If that describes you, don't worry. Chances are good that you can relate a later life experience that fits the Turn of Fortune scheme of things. What matters most is how this early life experience is playing out in the "here and now." We will explore that more in Chapter 12.

## Reflective Questions to Consider

1. Do you have a good idea of what your Turn of Fortune (age ten or earlier) was? If so, what was it that is so memorable for you?
2. If you don't have an idea of what your Turn of Fortune was, identify an event or experience after age 10 that fits the "Turn of Fortune" flow.

# 7

# The Spiritual Milestone

There is a spiritual lynchpin of sorts that unleashes a rush of insights to give us a foothold of understanding of the Personal Framework that surrounds our life. It's not the answer to everything, but it touches everything that is in the answer.

I have referred several times to the *Spiritual Milestone*, which is a specific and important Life Lesson. I have always conceptually understood that experiences are lessons and that we have the opportunity to learn and grow from them. Thank goodness we have the chance to learn in life and do better! Yet I somehow knew in my heart that my experience at age three was different from other Life Lessons in some way because it came up so often in the energy work I do. It was elevated somehow: a Life Lesson on steroids. This is the event I referred to in Chapter 6 when my mom almost died—my Turn of Fortune. This experience was central to my life journey, and like all Turns of Fortune, it pointed to a specific Life Lesson. I came to know the Life Lesson with my guides' help as a Spiritual Milestone of yearning.

Yearning is not a word I typically use, but it very quickly felt true to me. I *was* yearning. I have *always* been yearning. It is a longing that is sometimes front and center and other times like a heartbeat in the background of my life. This yearning has shown up for me in relationships (family, friendships, life partner), physical health, (weight, mobility, stamina), and purpose. Initially, I was surprised by the insight of this yearning. It was not in any way how I would describe myself. In fact, I viewed myself as generally fulfilled with some tweaking needed.

Very quickly, though, I passed through that block as the truth of it set in. In some way, it felt extremely liberating to understand this theme in my life, which gave context to my experience. It gathered up seemingly disparate events and put a bow around them. I was yearning. What surprised me most was that I didn't realize this underlying life theme before. I am a chronic over-thinker who spends a lot of time on self-development, yet this was beyond my reach. It was hidden in some way that I could not access. And, now, here it was.

This realization that I have maintained a state of yearning for most of my life fit with the significant life changes I experienced at the age of three. Because I felt so distraught about my family trauma, I yearned for a return to how things were when everyone was safe, happy, and together.

Wanting to learn more about the Spiritual Milestone, I peppered my guides with questions about it:

> Do I have more than one Spiritual Milestone? No
> Do I have other milestones of any sort? Yes
> What was I yearning for? Love and belonging
> Do all people have a Spiritual Milestone? Yes
> Are they all about yearning? No
> How many more types are there? Eleven

I spent the next several days being tutored by my guides about the concept of the Spiritual Milestone. It is a marker along a person's life journey that indicates spiritual growth is taking place. The Spiritual Milestone is determined in the pre-existence and is part of the Personal Framework. It first shows up in our lives as the particular challenge we're faced with in our Turn of Fortune and it is the second step in being infinite.

My Spiritual Milestone is yearning. Perhaps yours is angry. Or victimized. Or lacking. There are twelve types of Spiritual Milestones, but we work on only *one* Spiritual Milestone in a lifetime. My guides elaborated further, revealing that, on average, it takes many, many, many lifetimes to complete just one Spiritual Milestone. Before this lifetime, I have worked on the Spiritual Milestone of yearning in nineteen other lifetimes. My guides tell me people average ninety-five lifetimes to complete their Spiritual Milestone. The range is one to one hundred and one lifetimes. I have worked with clients at both extremes.

If you happen to be in the lifetime where you are working on the *last* of your twelve Spiritual Milestones, it has even more significance. This milestone is intended to be completed at a specific time within the lifetime. It is complex and it involves a heroic shift of consciousness.

Life Lessons represent the largest portion of the Personal Framework. Milestones are very big Life Lessons. The Spiritual Milestone is the biggest of the big and an underlying theme affecting many areas of our life.

---

### The 12 Spiritual Milestones are:

- lacking      inadequate in amount or degree
- separate      apart from others
- sad      showing sorrow or unhappiness
- guarded      cautious, wary, circumspect
- victimized      taken advantage of
- chaotic      a state of extreme confusion or disorder
- regretful      sense of loss over something done or undone
- shamed      a state of dishonor
- defenseless      lacking protection or support
- yearning      prolonged unfilled desire or need
- criticized      real or perceived flaws pointed out
- angry      strong emotion toward real/supposed grievance

---

Remember, you experience only *one* of these as a Spiritual Milestone during your lifetime. Though you will feel all of these things at some point in your life, you will experience one particularly intensely and consistently, and working through that dynamic will be key to your spiritual growth in terms of being infinite.

As I continued questioning my guides about Spiritual Milestones, I began to put together more pieces of the puzzle. For instance, there are significant benefits to your spirit's growth related to the Spiritual

Milestone, but none of those benefits are realized until *after* the milestone is complete. There is no partial credit along the way.

Benefits of completing the Spiritual Milestone include:

- alleviate suffering
- joyful progress toward self-love
- inspire creativity
- venture toward the Divine

Working through the Spiritual Milestone to completion is possible in any lifetime. In the lifetime in which the milestone is eventually completed, the average age of the person is age sixty-eight (range: ages thirty-nine to over one hundred). This suggests that completing the milestone happens with life experience.

Through this work and my Attracting Joy method, I have been able to complete my Spiritual Milestone and support many people in doing the same. I start by asking the Divine if I can be of help to the person in working on their milestone and completing it. If the person is far enough along in their Spiritual Milestone journey and with sufficient life experience, that permission may be granted. If permission is granted, I use the Attracting Joy method to work on it with them and confirm the Spiritual Milestone is complete.

When a person's Spiritual Milestone is finally made complete, there is no band that starts playing, no confetti that comes down from above, and no awards given. Perhaps that's all happening in another realm. When clients ask about what they should expect, I tell them the story of the goldfish in a small fish bowl. A clear glass divider was inserted down the middle of the fish bowl, allowing the fish to live, explore, and swim in only half of it. As the fish repeatedly bumped up against the glass partition, it began to avoid the barrier completely. After an extended time, the glass divider was removed from the bowl. The goldfish continue to swim *only* in the side he was used to. He did not test the boundaries after living so long in half the fish bowl. Despite the glass barrier being gone, the goldfish did not change his behavior.

This story is a reminder that even though the structural barrier or challenge of the Spiritual Milestone is gone, the person still needs to take the steps to explore what is now available to them. For me, what is available is a life with much less yearning! That said, yearning is not completely gone from my life—it simply doesn't have the gravitas it once did now that the milestone is complete. Once I understood the milestone, I found it helpful to welcome yearning into my life in some ways. It became something to understand and learn from, not hide away or deny.

Sometimes a person is not far enough along in the essential experience they need for their milestone to be completed with support. When that happens, we discuss the milestone as a theme in their life, and I encourage them to keep working on it. There is more on how to do this in Chapter 12. Simply understanding what our milestone is can be very helpful in working toward its completion.

Usually, people will look at the list of Spiritual Milestones and identify a few types that could be theirs. They often make a guess. Sometimes these guesses prove right (according to my guides), but they are always "close." For instance, one client thought her Spiritual Milestone was shamed. My guides helped us understand that her Spiritual Milestone was actually victimized, and shamed was a resulting emotion of the repeated victimization she experienced from others. This made great sense to her. Other times, though, people try to justify why their milestone must be something other than what it is. There can be a disavowal or attempted distancing of themselves from that which feels uncomfortable, foreign, and new. We will dive more deeply into this in Chapter 12 where I lead you through identifying your own Spiritual Milestone.

Why do we choose to become a human being? It is because we search for the answers to becoming more aligned with the Divine. As spirits, we can access our potential through the experiences of being human. It is through the Spiritual Milestone that this spiritual potential grows.

People do not need the help of energy work to complete their Spiritual Milestone, but the Attracting Joy methodology can support them in moving things along when appropriate.

When the Spiritual Milestone is completed, the graph of spiritual consciousness changes. Recall the "U curve" graph from Chapter 5, reprinted here.

# Spiritual Consciousness
## Average Person

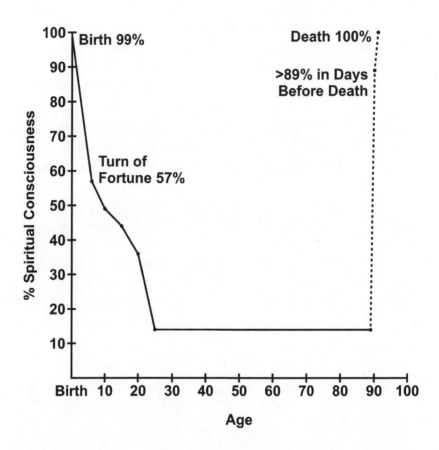

Significantly, the *ending* of the graph looks different once the Spiritual Milestone has been achieved

The graph in Figure 2 (page 49) represents a person who follows the early part of the first graph quite closely with the huge drop in percent of spiritual consciousness due to the Turn of Fortune. In addition, this person experienced another significant event in their early teens, dropping the percent of spiritual consciousness to a stabilizing level of about seventeen percent. It remained there until their mid-sixties, when it took a sharp turn upward to just under one hundred percent. This indicates the person completed their Spiritual Milestone. Remember, achieving the significant

Life Lesson of the Spiritual Milestone bumps the spiritual level up past discernment to the spiritual level of love, joy, or peace. That means the person in Figure 2 can experience life differently, and given their age, may have decades of life at this level.

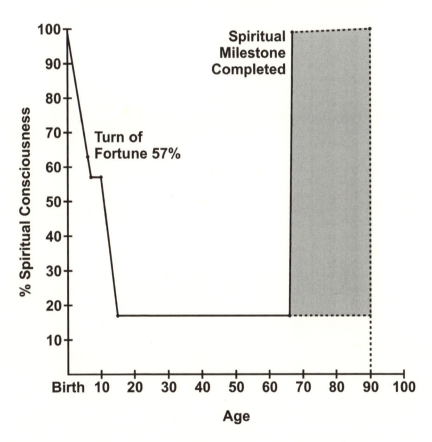

# Spiritual Consciousness with Spiritual Milestone Complete

Figure 2

My guides tell me that in the example above where the person's Spiritual Milestone is completed earlier in their life, upon passing away they exceed the level of spiritual consciousness with which they came into their life. This is optimal because it indicates they have experienced net positive spiritual growth through the process of being alive. The Divine wants us to complete our Spiritual Milestone so we may live the fullest life available to us.

## Reflective Questions to Consider

1. Did one of the twelve Spiritual Milestones resonate with you as your suspected milestone? Which one was it? Why?
2. Of the four benefits to completing your Spiritual Milestone, which appeals to you most right now?

- alleviate suffering
- joyful progress toward self-love
- inspire creativity
- venture toward the Divine

# 8

# Gathering Support

As we go through life, there are times when we realize just how much we rely on others. We give ourselves a lot of credit for what we have and who we are in life. We may have great ownership and pride in our story. There is, however, a broad interconnectedness that buoys us up that we often claim as ours alone. It comes in many forms: people who help or hinder us, resources that come our way serendipitously, or an economy that buoys us up or challenges us to make the success even sweeter. It comes in the way of having people enter our life who inspire us, teach us, encourage us, or challenge us in some way. It comes to us also through things happening in other parts of the world that we have no direct knowledge of but that create a ripple that finds its way to our personal shore. We have support around us that we are aware of and support that we are oblivious to. Gathering support is the third of the four steps to being infinite. There's power in becoming conscious of how and when we gather support and in accepting the role of providing support to others.

When my husband and I were dating, I transferred to a new plant to make our long-distance relationship a bit less long-distance. We went from living halfway across the country to just a few hours apart. What simplified the personal side of my life complicated the professional side. I stepped in to lead a business that was in crisis. All results areas had tanked with a new product initiative that was not fully developed technically. Though I was new to the site and this business group, I was immediately in the hot seat to turn things around. It was through an amazing group of managers and technicians rallying around this immense challenge that we wrestled the technical issues to the ground. In doing so, we built a capability and spirit that shifted our results from the dregs of the company to the top tier. There were so many things that made this some of the hardest work we'd ever done and the sweetest success we'd ever tasted.

Implicit in the turnaround was the collection of intentions of the players. Each person involved had in their Personal Framework and in their heart a drive to turn the chaos into success. Their capabilities and possibilities were called up and found a place in the whole that served both their personal development and the business' need. There was something about having "nothing to lose" that opened up our imaginations and allowed us to create unconventional solutions to accelerate change. For instance, production teams were re-structured to play to the strengths of the team members. A long-standing product design feature was challenged and changed. The boundaries of what we thought were limiting us were effectively changed by thinking differently about what was possible and simply going for it.

Successes in addressing structures and norms that were impeding us raised our confidence and our energy. They gave us a foothold to focus on the next thing that was in our way. The good work was showing up in our results, which only fueled group and individual determination to accelerate to the next purposeful goal. We were doing what needed to be done without pausing to second guess ourselves. We felt the urgency and were compelled to take extraordinary action.

There was no one player who made this remarkable, sustained turn-around happen. There weren't two or three or eight. It was a gathering of support that encompassed many people in the organization. The interdependencies were a strength that somehow still allowed each individual to shine, and the chaos that we came from evolved into the pride of the site. Through this trial came belonging and accomplishment.

Interdependency comes naturally to us. Somewhere in our adolescence (age range ten to fifteen), we opt out of this interconnectedness and put our faith in our self. This faith in self can propel us into distancing ourselves from support.

We are simply not meant to make this life journey alone. The universe is here to support us. It supports us in many ways unseen and unknown. Giving and receiving allows an exchange of love that lingers well beyond the act. It sustains us and extends far outside its origins. Using our guide teams is a perfect example of gathering support as we experience our life.

Even when we identify ourselves as proudly accomplishing something we have worked hard for, who among us can say we did it alone? No one. We are all products of a family, community, organization, state, country, and world. We are influenced by others along the way, sometimes by what they offer us and other times by what we reject. While we all have preferences of how we gather support in this life (Introvert? Extrovert? Lone wolf?), we are all gathering support in our own way. That is our free will, and it is worth confirming along the journey that our decisions of how we gather support are still serving us and others.

Support comes in many forms to aid in the Divine journey we take to grow our spirit. Even when we feel abandoned, we have support surrounding us through the assistance of our guides and other Divine beings who are asked by the Divine to offer help. Their love surrounds our heart and fortifies it with Divine blessings. Although your human suffering and difficulty may seem unending, your perseverance will be rewarded. Tap into that Divine love at the heart level when you doubt you have the support you seek. It will not go unanswered.

## Reflective Questions to Consider

1. Identify an event or experience in the past where you actively looked for other support in your area of biggest challenge. How might you expand even further to gather support for this challenge if it is still with you today?
2. Think of a recent time when you were asked by another person for support of some sort. How did you feel? Did you feel obliged? Did you feel honored?

# 9

# Consciousness

Life challenges such as the Turn of Fortune, the Spiritual Milestone, and the other Life Lessons are a vehicle for growing our consciousness. It is through these difficulties that we find new perspective, information, and truth. We begin to make connections we didn't see before. These connections often challenge our beliefs as we become aware of other points of view and experiences.

We may have a tendency to be complacent when it comes to self-growth. It is easy and often encouraged to stay put, to not rock the boat, and to not question what we think we know to be true. This is one of the reasons we may resist experiences such as these, even though we ultimately benefit from them.

For many years I was a staff member on a wonderful transformational workshop titled "People Supporting People." My employer offered it to employees to help further our personal development as well as our appreciation and understanding of the impacts and value of diversity in the workplace. This workshop was the real deal: it was unlike anything I had experienced before.

The workshop had thirty to forty attendees, including representation from every level of the organization. There were managers and hourly workers. Some participants were newly hired and others almost retired. Every ethnicity in the company was represented. There were people with Ivy League educations and high school diplomas. There was gender diversity. And that was just the visible diversity--the diversity of our life experiences was also with us.

There are times in our lives when we find ourselves in a profound learning environment. It is as if the universe conspired to allow a transformational shift to occur and we are willing participants. There are also times when we deny ourselves the shift available to us.

The workshop was ingeniously designed. It very quickly created a safe space and encouraged participants to be authentic and share deeply. This approach was role modeled by staff and there were always a few brave souls who trusted quickly and went deep just as quickly. That nudged those who were less sure of the process to give it a try. The exercises were thought provoking and beautiful. The setting gave people the time and space to gift themselves true reflection and insight.

After that powerful look within, the workshop guided the participants to explore further outside themselves with exercises that explored aspects of human behavior, development, and diversity. We were then asked again to share deeply and by that point, everyone was willing. For instance, we asked every person to share a time when they experienced discrimination and how it felt. One by one, every participant shared. It was heartbreaking. The stories were real and the emotions were raw, no matter how many years had passed.

As a staff member, each time I went through this experience I knew I was going to learn something profound and difficult. Each time I heard the stories of economic, social, racial, gender, and sexual orientation discrimination that were experienced by these people I now knew, my understanding deepened further. My consciousness was raised. It expanded. It was not an intellectual thing, but simultaneously emotional, cognitive, physical, and spiritual instead. People spoke from their heart, from their pain, and from their vulnerability.

Consciousness is a deep awareness. It is a deep understanding. It is a connecting rod in the psyche that joins things in a way that were never joined before. Expanded consciousness helps us to move forward with our senses engaged but in a very different way.

Consciousness is the ever-expanding relationship to the ever-expanding consciousness of all beings connected to Divine love. Consciousness comes through this connection to Divine love. The Divine guides us to truth unrestricted by the limitations of our human beliefs. It is through this truth that consciousness grows.

I asked my guides about consciousness and they said, "Consciousness contradicts dishonor." Becoming more conscious is a way of honoring ourselves and each other. As I thought about that, Dr. Maya Angelou's quote, "When you know better, you do better," came to mind. I asked my guides if that's another way of saying "consciousness contradicts dishonor." They said yes.

When you know better, you do better. When *I* know better, *I* do better. When I knew better about how behaviors and situations affected the people in that workshop, I began to do better.

When I think of this rather simple concept, I am reminded of my weight problem, which has really not been simple for me at all. I first became aware of my weight as an issue in middle school. It became increasingly more concerning to me through high school and has remained a source of angst ever since. At this point, it feels like *the* thing that holds me back from feeling truly successful.

It seems strange that this issue has such impact. It is in my Personal Framework and appears to be the best way to get and keep my attention on following through to do the work of Attracting Joy and this book I have been drawn to write.

In the realm of knowing better/doing better, I know a *lot* about how to reduce my weight. I know how to count calories, fat grams, protein, and fiber. I know how important it is to drink enough water and sleep well. I know the importance of exercise. I know it's good to avoid processed foods and limit refined sugar. That is a fraction of what I know intellectually about being a healthy weight.

When it comes to my weight, I know better, but I don't do better. Why is that?

My guides tell me the answer lies in two areas: Life Lessons and consciousness.

For me, Life Lessons are responsible for about fifty-five percent of my weight issue and consciousness is about forty-five percent. Twelve of my sixteen life lessons are connected to my weight issue. No wonder this has been a challenge! I have worked on those Life Lessons by simply living my life and with the help of the Attracting Joy method where needed. That attended to, let's move on to consciousness.

Consciousness is who I am right now. It is the sum total of all the choices I have made in my life encapsulated into the present. My unique consciousness is the center of gravity of all the disparate choices I have made to date in all areas of my life. It guides my reactions, emotions, and behaviors, all in one untidy package.

While my consciousness is the sum total of all the choices I have made in my life, my consciousness also impacts my choices *today*. Consciousness, or awareness, includes what I choose to believe, what I study, how I observe, how I relate to others, and how I make decisions. Consciousness can be very limited with distinct boundaries. This is where awareness of incapacity comfortably resides. This consciousness is generally not supportive of connecting to the infinite self.

In contrast, consciousness can be very expansive with few boundaries. It can be infinite. This is where our genius emerges to help us see the infinite routes to expanding consciousness and improving our world.

We move along a continuum of consciousness between these two extremes over the course of our lifetime. Where we might be restrictive in our consciousness in one area of our lives, it is possible to be open and expansive in another area. My guides tell me that most often we remain in a very small section of the consciousness continuum during our lifetime, although it is possible to make giant leaps of consciousness. Regarding my weight, I would say I have occupied a very small section of the consciousness continuum.

We experience our lives often through our interactions with others. These interactions are a great determinant of consciousness, and our consciousness determines how we interact with others. It is an endless loop. Relationships engage us, enthrall us, frustrate us, limit us, help us breakthrough to new possibilities, and sometimes keep us stuck where we are. Just as we are operating in and through our consciousness, others are too. Their consciousness journey has the potential to either stimulate our own consciousness' growth and expansion or to limit us to retreating further.

Who we are right now is not all there is available to us. There are myriad possibilities beyond the "here and now". We may choose again to have a different outcome, to change the otherwise inevitable trajectory of the moment and of our lives. Will we resist the pull of the ego's limitations for the lovely subtle energy of the Divine? That is available to us now. It is always available to us.

Change in life comes from a change in consciousness. We can develop our consciousness in the direction of our dreams. We are free to choose, and when we have made a choice that no longer serves us (or never did), we can choose again.

When we consider how much positivity can arise through our decision to change course and boldly seek to expand our awareness, we can begin the process of connecting with our greatest and highest good. This is what the Divine makes available to us all.

The magnitude of the countless choices, large and small, that we have made weigh the scales of the future to make it likely that it's similar to our past—that is, unless we make a change. We may choose to veer from our current trajectory. We may look in another place for inspiration and new possibility. We may open our hearts to the Divine.

So…back to my weight and the role consciousness plays in the journey.

What is it that eludes me? What am I missing? If consciousness is the sum total of our experiences, I decided to look at what my experiences tell me about my weight.

What is the dynamic that keeps us from a goal we strongly desire? What draws us away from what we worked so hard to achieve or keeps us from achieving it in the first place? What compels us to act in ways that don't serve us—when some force within seems determined to override our best intentions? The answer lies with a concept called "attractor fields." We'll explore that next.

## Reflective Questions to Consider

1. Is there a stubborn or chronic issue in your life from which you would like to learn? What is that issue? What have you learned so far?
2. Transformational change is a big idea. What draws you toward taking the leap? What stops you from moving forward?

# 10

## Attractor Fields

The Divine wants us to be happy and on some level we have what we need to be happy. Even though we are set up for success, there are influences that make this difficult as we live our life on this Earth. Although there are many types of influences, the most significant is attractor fields.

I define an *attractor field* as focused energy that activates behavior. Multiple events, experiences, and emotions energetically connect to form our attractor fields. Some of these fields are clearly significant to us and others are seemingly insignificant. Some we recall, others we don't. They get layered on over time, very naturally building in significance as we grow up and grow older. They become what Dr. David R. Hawkins, author of *Power vs. Force*, calls "profoundly powerful patterns that organize human behavior." Attractor fields influence our health, relationships, work, choices, and ambitions.

Even though we like to think we are able to determine our own destiny, we are subject to many influences that drive our behavior and impact what choices we make. Our free will only takes us so far when it comes to the influence of attractor fields.

Let's take a look at a common phenomenon with which we are all familiar: gravity. Although we seldom think about it, the gravitational field of our planet affects many aspects of life. It keeps us predictably interacting with our environment in specific ways. For instance, we can take a walk in the autumn woods and not worry about floating off into space, and if we trip over a tree root on that walk, we know we'll either fight to keep our balance or fall down. Even the colorful leaves fluttering to the ground offer subtle reminders of the force of gravity. Simply put, gravity is a given, and it's a powerful attractor field.

While gravity is an earthly attractor field, our lives are also impacted by attractor fields that affect us individually and in groups. They are the products of our thoughts, experiences, beliefs, life events, and culture. Attractor fields form as we go through life and affect how we make decisions about how to interact with the world. Though Life Lessons are a given, our attractor fields pull us in the direction of certain experiences that contain the Life Lessons we came here to learn. Once we are conscious of this, we can influence our attractor fields through our thoughts and beliefs and begin to (roughly) steer ourselves toward certain experiences or outcomes.

Significant life events for each of us include our awareness of incapacity, or conclusion that we are not good enough in some way. These are turning points of the spirit, consciousness, and the mortal self that can be triggered by any of the following:

- fear
- panic
- humiliation
- abuse

This is where the ego begins to hold more sway in our lives and our connection to our spirit lessens.

For me, one very important example was at age three with the significant unexpected change in the connection with my mom over that critical period. The safe, predictable world I'd known changed dramatically and this launched one of my powerful attractor fields: the need to control. In addition to that attractor field of control, my guides tell me thirty-nine other attractor fields initiated at age three. All thirty-nine were challenges to overcome, and all of them are still with me today, though at a different level than where they started.

It's important to note that attractor fields can be positive or negative, powerful or forceful, strong or weak. They are not static. Attractor fields are reinforced by the processes of living. My attractor field of needing to control didn't do much for me as a middle child and the family dynamic, but it served me well in academics.

I loved school. I loved the predictability of it: seeing my friends, learning, and the sameness of the Monday through Friday routine appealed to me. I soon learned that getting good grades got me positive attention at home.

The first reward I remember for getting good grades was food. When I was in second grade, my dad brought me home a little bag of cheese popcorn from work for my report card. I remember it like it was yesterday. I was surprised by the unexpected gesture and I loved receiving special attention from my hardworking dad. This reinforced my efforts at school, and my studious habits became a positive, strong and powerful aspect of my need to control. Conversely, my connection of "food as a reward" was not quite as positive.

My guides tell me that a whopping fifty-one attractor fields influence my consciousness and contribute at some level to my weight issue: forty-one are negative, forceful fields and ten are positive, powerful ones that are not fully optimized. No wonder it has been a challenge!

The work is to neutralize the forceful negative fields and optimize the powerful positive fields. Both can be achieved in many ways. I addressed mine through my Attracting Joy method.

Attractor fields cannot be shed like an old habit, but they can be transformed. These fields have a "continuum of potential" ranging from a very low, undesirable level to a very high, desirable level. In my work with the Attracting Joy method, I use a range of zero to one thousand. For example, love and hate are two extremes of the same idea: hate occupies the low end of the range and love occupies the high end of the range. The continuum in between these extremes includes shades of those ideas. It's like a sliding scale, with the low vibration of the ego at the low end and the high vibration of spirit at the high end.

There are a great many examples of this type of continuum. Here are a few more:

- skepticism.....trust
- fear.....confidence

- miserable…..contented
- grief…..delight
- unworthy…..valuable

For example, in the environment of a social gathering, I may trust myself around alcohol but be skeptical I will resist the temptation of the appetizers. In terms of energy work, I may have a high level of confidence in my ability to help others, but a fear I will not be able to help myself when it comes to my weight. Throughout my life I may be contented in my relationship with my guides but miserable in my relationship with food. When exploring hobbies such as kayaking, I may feel delight in paddling a kayak and grief at the prospect of how I look getting into the kayak.

Let's take a look at my weight and those fifty-one attractor fields. Attractor fields come from our life experience and so any difficult life experience is a likely place to look for insight into my weight. For me, let's go back to age three.

My family trauma at my age three resulted in forty negative attractor fields. Of those negative attractor fields, seven directly affected my weight. Here's how:

## Age three weight-related attractor fields:

- panic
- vulnerability
- grief
- lack of control
- unsupported
- self-abuse
- worthlessness

Over the years, the list of weight-related attractor fields grew much longer, though typically only by one or two attractor fields at a time. Age thirty-nine became another big trauma year for me. This time, the catalyst involved my career.

I had a new assignment managing the largest operation at our manufacturing plant. It came on the heels of a real success story as described in Chapter 8, where my challenging role in another operation created a complete turnaround of all key business results. I loved that role and the people that I worked with to produce such amazing results. In addition to feeling hard-earned pride in our accomplishments, I experienced a tremendous feeling of belonging while there.

My reward for a job well done was another high-profile assignment, and I was excited about it. Things did not go well, however, and when business results suffered, I did, too. The two things in life that drive me to feel successful are to achieve and to belong. If either of those things are present, my life is good. If both are present (as they were in my previous role), my life is great. If neither is present, life feels very, very hard. In this role, we were unsuccessful on the results front, *and* I never felt a sense of belonging in the organization. It was awful.

This was unusual for me. The result was also an outlier in my professional life: having failed in my role as the leader, I was removed and placed in a site-wide support role. The pain of this failure was palpable, and I spent the next three years healing my wounded pride and rebuilding my reputation.

In my subsequent Attracting Joy reflections and investigations, I learned that I initiated twenty-nine more attractor fields—twenty-two negative and seven positive—during that time. Ten of those negative attractor fields played a role in my continued and increasing issue with weight. Here's the list:

## Age thirty-nine weight-related attractor fields:

- defensiveness
- my efforts not received as intended
- shock
- shame
- taken for granted
- confusion
- depression
- conflict
- heartache
- insecurity

I worked very hard in that high-profile role to get the expected business results and to build a strong team. Although I could point to many reasons why we were unsuccessful, the call was made to make a change in leadership. In hindsight, I now think it was a good decision. It was done in a caring way. A structural change was made to make the next candidate more successful. Yet I still felt terrible about letting the organization and myself down.

While these ten attractor fields were initially low vibration, negative and forceful, I was able to eventually transition them to the high vibration, positive and powerful side of the continuum by use of the Attracting Joy method. Here is how these seventeen weight-related attractor fields transformed:

| Age three weight-related attractor field | What it became |
|---|---|
| • panic | assurance |
| • vulnerability | determination |
| • grief | joy |
| • lack of control | relief |
| • unsupported | supported |
| • self-abuse | self-love |
| • worthless | worthy |

| Age thirty-nine weight-related attractor field | What it became |
|---|---|
| • defensiveness | benefit |
| • efforts not received as intended | appreciated |
| • shock | wonder |
| • shame | dignity |
| • taken for granted | recognized |
| • confusion | order |
| • depression | happiness |
| • conflict | harmony |
| • heartache | hopefulness |
| • insecurity | courage |

The new takes on those old negative attractor fields breathed life into new possibilities and ease with my weight. The original seventeen low vibrational attractor fields outlined above were part of only two events in my life.

Today, simply looking at each of the columns of words above feels entirely different and brings me a new frame of mind, creating a whole new energy level and approach for this challenge.

The complexity of the attractor field discussion doesn't stop here. Attractor fields can have many different aspects, affecting multiple areas of our life and in nuanced ways. For instance, the "grief" field for my weight at age three ultimately rose to "joy." But, through my life, I've had three other grief fields pop up. Here's how they showed up:

| Age | Situation | Low vibration to positive vibration |
| --- | --- | --- |
| nineteen | college | grief rose to encouragement |
| forty-six | surgery | grief rose to content |
| fifty-nine | father died | grief rose to well-being |

The age nineteen college grief had to do with dropping a class, thereby challenging my belief I was a good student. The age forty-six surgery grief attractor field undermined my healthy self-image, and I explained the grief of my father dying in Chapter 3. The variety of experiences prompting the same emotion shows that grief comes in many forms.

Attractor fields are like a backdrop of our life because we often don't realize they are there. Other times we know they were there but think they've been resolved. An example from my life dates to age nineteen and my sophomore year at Michigan Tech.

As mentioned earlier, I loved school and always excelled. My first year studying engineering went very well, but suddenly in my second year I was about to fail physics. What? Just a few weeks into the term, while prepping for a big exam, my initial confidence about the material quickly drained away. I realized I didn't have a clue, and I panicked. That had never happened to me before. The test was a week away, but the last day to drop the class was before that. I knew in my heart I couldn't catch up in time given my class load, so I made the difficult decision to drop my physics class. I know people drop college classes all the time, but this is the only time it ever happened to me. More importantly, I was stunned by how ill-prepared I was.

I felt like such a failure. I questioned if I was at the right university and in the right degree program. All sorts of negative beliefs bubbled to the surface. I felt like I wasn't good enough. I felt a separation from my classmates who seemed to be ready for the test. I knew dropping the class likely meant adding another year to my degree program. How would I explain this to my parents or reconcile this with my self-image of being a great student? I fell into deep grief and a new attractor field was born.

In hindsight, dropping physics turned out to be a good decision. I did great in the rest of my classes that term. I aced physics during the next term, getting right back on the horse that bucked me off. And through some creative scheduling and hard work, I still graduated in four years. The situation was humbling but I made it through. End of story, right?

Not quite. That attractor field of grief still held sway in my life. It remained a low vibrational field with the ability to impact me. I was likely to re-experience it. It made me question whether I could really count on the things I thought were "solid." What if another unexpected failure loomed in my future?

And, of course, all of this came to the fore again with the humbling business failure at age thirty-nine, and was made all the worse because it came on the heels of a spectacular success.

Clearly, the grief dynamic was still there.


## Re-experiencing

As human beings we experience difficulty on many levels in our lives. This can range from the merely inconvenient to the tragic. Some things we can easily resolve and let pass, while others have real staying power. What happens with those events that we just can't shake? We re-experience them.

Re-experience involves a mental attachment that is unconscious and does not allow forward movement. It is much more than simply a hurtful memory, bitterness, or a grudge. We mentally attach to a negative experience when there is trauma, fear, and separation of some sort. When all three are present, it imprints in a way that is indelible.

My guides tell me that everyone experiences this at least once, and at most fifteen times. On average, a person has five such re-experience issues. I had seven. Re-experiencing is a means to help us resolve the original experience.

Unsurprisingly, my first issue was my challenge at age three. My Turn of Fortune was the initiating event and was re-experienced about six months later although in less dramatic fashion. The original trauma of being present while my mother was bleeding profusely, the fear that I felt from other family members, and the separation from my immediate family until she was back home all coupled to create a re-experience scenario several months later. I was grieving.

Through this experience, I eventually worked around this grief in two ways. The first was seeking love and recognition through others. The second was a strong desire to please others. They served as a substitute for my grief: an action plan to avoid grief that only shifted how it was experienced.

This showed up strongly in my need as a small child to be a "good girl." Following the rules was praised, so I was all about doing that to gain favor with my parents. Good grades brought a smile to their faces and individual recognition, reinforcing my efforts. Because I knew I could become a casualty of circumstances beyond my control, I tried whatever I could to stay in their good graces. I didn't want to be left behind again. I wanted to be easy to have around. I wanted to be loved and my way to do it was to people-please.

That's why as an adult, when I was pulled from a key career assignment for performance reasons, I was devastated. It did not fit my self-image of a good girl/people pleaser and I had a lot of healing to do as a result. I literally felt like I was rebuilding my self-worth from the ground up.

Several years later, I felt like I was on top again from the standpoint of career performance and I opted to retire early. One of my biggest challenges was how to tell my parents that I was leaving this stable, prestigious, well-paying job with no specific plan. Even though my husband and I were financially secure, I knew how proud my parents were of me in that position and I didn't want to disappoint them. When I told them my news, they were delighted for me and excited about what came next. All the angst and dread I felt in telling them was wasted energy, but my people-pleasing grief work-around was running the show.

Often the energetic burden of an event carries on and we re-experience it, whether in ways that are similar (recognizable) or dis-similar (related, but in a different form). The energetic shadow of the event lingers in ways that deter us from healing fully.

Many people learn what they need and are able to heal through talking with trusted friends, family, and counselors. Others work to plow through it on their own, perhaps never speaking of it with another person. Some may self-medicate. Many may pray. Others may meditate. Some may enlist the help of an energy worker.

A good indication we have not fully learned the lesson from a particular life event is intense sudden emotion, which many people call "triggers." These can happen in an instant. Perhaps you are triggered by a scene in a movie, a conversation with a parent, or the telling of a story. When it happens, we are surprised and often have a difficult time regaining our composure. We then have the choice to simply stuff it down and pretend it didn't affect us or to recognize and take steps to further heal the situation that we thought we had already healed.

There are many ways to cut the cord of re-experiencing. Here are some of them:

- Forgiving self and others
- Focusing on love
- Gathering support from others for help
- Severing our connection from the event(s)
- Divine assistance

These can be addressed consciously by focusing on them and working through them cognitively, through prayer and meditation, and by energy modalities like Attracting Joy. Being freed from this re-experiencing allows you to more easily be in the present moment and living in the "here and now" instead of reliving the past through today's experiences.

Some twenty years after re-experiencing this grief attractor field that originated at age nineteen, I used the Attracting Joy method to address that old grief and transform it to a positive, high vibrational and powerful counterpart: "encouragement." This manifested as a sense of confidence and closure for these difficult chapters in my life.

Attractor fields can be a force for building us up, tearing us down, or both, as in the case of a negative attractor field being resolved and the power of understanding it. They affect us not only as individuals, but as a part of groups and even cultures when they are born of common experiences. Despite the common origin, they are processed uniquely based on our Personal Framework and level of consciousness. As our consciousness expands, our ability to address our negative attractor fields increases.

## Reflective Questions to Consider

1.  Do you feel the pull of negative attractor fields in a particular struggle? Describe it.
2.  My guides said that everyone experiences "re-experiencing" at least once, and at most fifteen times. Identify one of your re-experiencing occasions. Does it still have a hold on you today?

# 11

# Trust

Life gives us the chance to determine where we will flourish. We can decide how we engage with people, places, and things so that we see (somewhat) how our mortal decisions fare in the world in which we live. Sometimes we find ourselves smack-dab in the middle of a situation that showcases how our free will interacts with our attractor fields. This chapter addresses the fourth step to becoming infinite: trust. We will explore this fourth step of trust through concepts that are part of our Personal Framework as the "eternal stimulus." Recall the eternal stimulus prods us to evolve and transform. It is the Divine drive that spurs us into action as we take form as a human being. It is an integral part of our human experience.

Although we are largely influenced by attractor fields as part of our consciousness, there is of course room for breaking free from their influence. Free will, after all, is an important Life Lesson for each of us. How else could we possibly expect to expand and connect with our infinite self? Patterns may be strong, but they are not unchangeable.

## The Essence

In my late twenties I was responsible for a manufacturing area within my company. The decision was made by the corporate Business Team to consolidate our operation into other plants to simplify the supply chain and save money. This approach was happening not only in my business, but company-wide and globally, changing the face of much of the manufacturing model.

I knew the numbers. I understood the strategy. I knew that all of us—myself and my employees—would not be laid off and would move on to jobs in other parts of the plant. I also knew I would be rewarded for quietly and competently transitioning the production elsewhere and shutting down our operation.

And I knew in my heart it was the wrong decision. I felt that very strongly. I was a low-level manager with six years of work experience, all with this Fortune 25 company. Despite the powerlessness of my position, it became my mission to get this decision changed.

This newly-found mission was not "like me." I am a rule-follower and was supportive of the overall company strategy…that was my job, after all, and I was good at it. Despite that, when it came to *this* shutdown decision, I could not support it. I worked my concern up the chain of command. Eventually, I contacted my manager's manager's manager and asked to be put on the agenda at the next corporate Business Team meeting. Though I had never participated in a Business Team meeting before, I travelled to the meeting at corporate headquarters and made my case, using data and my personal passion to convince them to change course. They listened politely but were unconvinced. The decision to shut us down was firm.

I tried again, this time insisting that the Business Team come to our operation and see it for themselves. This was a bold and unprecedented request. They didn't feel it necessary. I insisted they owed it to our organization to see what they would be giving up. Over the previous few years our team, technology, and results developed in ways that were compelling and that I knew were not present or readily available at the other facilities. I called our Division Manager to ask for his support in getting them to come. This also was a bold and unprecedented request. Surprisingly, he made it happen.

The Business Team flew in on a corporate jet one morning and stayed for several hours, hearing what was compelling about our operation not from me, but from the hourly technicians that ran the place. I was the stage mom off in the wings. My team was powerful in their understanding of their equipment and processes and the overall business. They were effective in conveying their dedication authentically and with conviction.

On their flight back, the Business Team reversed its decision to shut us down and the business enjoyed several more years of excellence. We promised big and delivered even bigger in production and service from our plant.

My role leading this effort was a big gamble and it was certainly outside my comfort zone to do anything other than what I was told. But this time, I was inspired to do something very different. I knew it might be detrimental to my career and get me the kind of attention that wasn't desirable. It was a high risk/high reward situation that ended up working out great for the company, the business, and for me.

This is an example of trust and the Divine drive to evolve and transform. Though we are greatly influenced by attractor fields or patterns that guide and even predict human behavior, it is possible and necessary to move beyond those influences that keep us from moving forward—that keep us from expanding and connecting with our infinite self.

There is that beautiful core of the Divine connection that is always present in us: *the essence.* It's more than a connection, though. The essence is a Divine bond of creativity and transfiguration. It is what gives us courage to take creative steps to see and live our lives differently. It can change the course of our life.

The essence is the Divine within each of us. It is not just part of us— at our core, it *is* us. We are Divine. We tend to identify much more with our mortal life and experiences than we do our Divinity, but it is there. It is always there and available for us to make creative choices that lead to transfiguration. That is the key to our Life Lessons, our Personal Framework, our growth in this lifetime, and of our spirit's growth. It's connecting to our infinite self, and it increases our contribution to Divine expansion.

Being one with our essence spurs creativity and allows transfiguration to take place. It can happen in a moment. We can get a glimpse of this, like I was blessed to have experienced at age twenty-nine for the three-month period this occurred. My guides tell me about thirty-nine million people on earth have experienced being "one with their essence" in their own way at some point in time. In a world population of 7.8 billion people, that's about half a percent.

I asked my guides how this glimpse of being one with the essence happens. They said it happens when these four things are aligned: the grace of God, the state of our essence, the level of our spirit, and trust.

I did not know at the time of my experience that this was going on. Yet as I reflect on that time, I see that it was unique in my life. Once I got clear that shutting us down was something I didn't support, I felt like everything that I was doing—all those brash requests of the organization—had a tail wind. I felt such certainty despite the odds.

Before the Business Team visit, my plant manager encouraged me to commit to saving two million dollars for the business during the visit. He thought that might tip the scales in our favor. I agreed. During the visit, though, I didn't do it.

I remember him waiting for me to announce it during our closing meeting with the Business Team. His body language was urging me. I didn't do it—not because I didn't think we could save two million dollars, but because I wanted to let our proposal stand on its own. Although we got the outcome we were looking for and we weren't shutting down, my plant manager asked me a few weeks later why I didn't commit to the two million dollars the way he asked me to. I told him doing so would minimize what was really possible. It was a drop in the bucket. He believed me.

My plant manager could have easily interpreted me not announcing that two million in savings as not having the guts to commit to something big. He might have viewed me as a wild card. It didn't turn out that way. He accepted my explanation, and I was promoted within months, much earlier than was the norm. In that time and in that place and with the grace of God, my essence, my spirit, and trust, I was connecting with my infinite self and the universe cooperated.

## Intention

Even when we commit ourselves fully to something that matters to us, there is something more that we can do to ensure we are on our way to being infinite. Our intention is the key to making our desire whole and it is fully within our control. We strengthen our intention through offering our love gladly and holding the love given to us as a sacred gift. Our intention manifests our desires in accordance with the Divine direction.

Because we are spiritual beings having a human experience, our intention must include the spirit as well as our humanity. That is, we must move in wholeness and with an intention of wholeness to fully reach that which we seek.

## Wholeness

Accepting the ego is necessary for wholeness. We often refer to the ego with disdain. The ego is very misunderstood. It is not our enemy, nor is it something to overcome. It is, however, a side of us that demands our attention. The ego allows us to see and experience the low frequency side of things so we can fully exchange that mistaken belief that we are inadequate with the knowledge we are all one. There is a lightness aspect to the ego that often goes unnoticed but is always with us. There is an opportunity to shift the ego from the darkness to the light. It is our destiny to reconcile this understanding in a way that soothes the embattled ego. This is done through recognizing the importance of this lesson and honoring the role the ego plays in our life.

What helps us reconcile with the extremes of the ego's range is our willingness to engage with the lighter side of the ego. We do this by noticing the side of us that simply wants to be heard but is drowned out by the ego demanding "look here, not there." There is a loveliness of the ego that wants what is best for us and honors our free will.

## Shifting into Spiritual Harmony

Much of life is about finding our way to spiritual harmony so we can offer the very best of who we are to the world. Even when we know what we are doing is hurting others, we seek in our hearts to move toward love of them and ourselves. In general, the majority of our life (fifty-six percent) is spent in disharmony. It is our relationship with our spirit that offers us a way to break the pattern of discord that keeps us from loving fully. This spiritual relationship is the goal of our lifetime.

Each of us has a relationship with our spirit. It is an uneasy alliance. We see ourselves as separate from our spirit because we wish to have complete autonomy and independence. This is a route to nowhere. It is our connections to our spirit and to others that is our way to being infinite. These relationships to all sources of the Divine serve to lift us up to our greatest and highest good. We simply cannot be infinite without them.

This is not a solitary journey. The dark side of our ego would have us believe it is. We try time and time again to hold ourselves apart from the very thing that is our salvation. Allow the love of your spirit to grow through every interaction with everyone you meet. Seek out the beauty of the people in your life. You will see it if you look for it. The beauty of their essence will support your own. You may be surprised how your love of all things transforms your love of yourself.

By loving yourself you shift into loving your spirit. Conversely, it's precisely this harmony with your spirit that allows you to love yourself. It is a spiral of infinite possibility and infinite clarity of connection to the Divine. This illumination allows certainty in knowing how to navigate life's journey and allows mindful spiritual peace to prevail. We all know how challenging it is to become our most centered, authentic, connected selves. Our connection to our spirit makes this a natural way of being. Spiritual harmony opens us up to a life of joy.

Spiritual harmony is a shift we make when we move through the challenging events of our lives in a way that fully embraces the spirits of everyone involved. It's when we can see past the mask of the individual and connect with the essence of who they are. The world does not encourage this. The Divine does. It is as if we can only be infinite through the full acceptance of our imperfect, messy, inglorious life. We are not here to escape difficulty. We are here to find our way to spiritual harmony despite that difficulty. Challenges will continue to unfold in our lives in ways we cannot anticipate, but by asking the Divine to shift us into harmony with the spirit that is with us, we can find meaning and peace in everything that comes our way.

Trust is necessary as a step to being infinite because it allows the giant steps forward beyond what we know. It is the eternal stimulus and our free will in action, and it propels us through and beyond the atmosphere of our attractor fields toward our greatest and highest good.

## Reflective Questions to Consider

1. Have you noticed the side of you that simply wants to be heard but is drowned out by the ego? When did that last happen for you? Why do you think it happened then?
2. How do you handle the challenges to become your most centered, authentic, connected self?

# 12

# What's MY Spiritual Milestone?

One of the ways we can shift into spiritual harmony is by recognizing the patterns in our lives that keep us from doing so. These patterns follow a theme of vulnerability that is ours to work through via life experiences.

Have you ever thought about what motivates you to choose one thing over another? I attended a class many years ago that addressed the concept of choice and how it relates to the basic needs of human beings. In addition to basic safety/security, the other basic needs according to Dr. William Glasser's Control Theory are:

- Power/Accomplishment
- Belonging/Love
- Freedom
- Fun

We all have all of these needs but typically one or two of them are dominant. In the class, we did an exercise to determine which need was dominant.

For me, power/accomplishment was dominant followed closely by belonging/love. Knowing this was helpful in understanding what was missing at times in my life when I was unhappy or dissatisfied. For instance, if I was in a team environment where my power and belonging needs were both met, I was in my high-performance pattern, got a lot done, and felt great about it. As a bonus, freedom and fun came along for the ride. This was where breakthrough happened, like my age twenty-nine business shutdown example.

If I was in a team where power *or* belonging was present, but not both, I was generally feeling pretty good about things. This is where I have spent most of my life. If *neither* power nor belonging was present, my life felt like an abject failure and freedom and fun were nowhere to be found. This example was my age thirty-nine business failure. When this happened, I needed to develop a plan to address both power and belonging to turn the situation around. I found it extremely helpful knowing what my basic needs were to focus my efforts. If I didn't, I might be tempted to search for freedom and fun, which could meet a short term need but not help me in the long run.

Just like it was helpful for me in my thirties to understand what drove my decisions, decades later I found it very helpful to understand my life theme of yearning as my Spiritual Milestone. Simply *knowing* my Spiritual Milestone gave me renewed insight into the context of my life.

In the spirit of consciousness and knowing better/doing better, this chapter is devoted to helping you determine your own Spiritual Milestone as well as other contributing factors to the Turn of Fortune. There are several ways to do this. For instance, you can contact an energy practitioner who has familiarity with this "be infinite" work and ask for their help. Perhaps you have a strong relationship with your guides and you can ask them directly. You can pray or meditate about it. You can also do an easy Do-It-Yourself method using the process outlined in this chapter.

I like the DIY method. Why? Because it asks you to figuratively get your hands dirty. This tool requires personal reflection and evaluation of specific times in your life that only *you* have experienced. Given that, at its conclusion, what you find should also make sense to you. If it doesn't, you can try to gather support as suggested in Chapter 8. This will help you process your Spiritual Milestone with people who know you.

For example, I brought the above mentioned exercise to a group of managers to try. One woman was disappointed when her dominant need was freedom. She thought it would be power/accomplishment. She *wanted* it to be power/accomplishment because that was what seemed to be valued most at the company. When she shared it with her co-workers who knew her well, they unanimously reinforced that freedom was her dominant need based on their experience with her. Eventually, she came to better understand her need for freedom, embraced it, and felt good about making a career change more aligned with her needs. Understanding her need for freedom was freeing!

There is no good or bad judgment of any of the four basic needs. They simply are what they are. That will hold true for the Spiritual Milestone and the other exercises as well. The opportunity is not in simply knowing which need or Spiritual Milestone we have, but in developing our ability to recognize and use it in a way that serves us.

## The Process

For the DIY approach to identifying your Spiritual Milestone, please refer to the Spiritual Milestone Worksheet (Figure 3, page 81). To download the worksheet, visit www. Sallyheidtke.com. In this section, we'll walk through the process together. I recommend setting aside at least a half hour to complete the exercise where and when you will not be disturbed.

The heart of the process is doing a mini "life review" and identifying the difficult life events that have challenged you. Difficult life experiences can be listed as an overall topic, or you may break them down into separate events. For instance, on my life review I listed "broke leg sledding" and "third grade alone at lunch" as two separate issues. I could have combined them. Either way is fine, but you need at least twelve events in your worksheet. Breaking down larger or more complex events may be helpful in discerning distinctly different aspects of a protracted situation. The list doesn't need to be chronological, though many people find that helps them remember things.

You may have more that the requested number of difficult life events you could include and if that's the case, select those about which you feel most strongly. That will be sufficient to determine your milestone. Typically, the longer you have lived the easier this part of the exercise is as there is usually more to choose from.

## Spiritual Milestone Exercise

Date:

1   List 15 or more difficult life events that you personally experienced (directly or indirectly). Take your time.

2   For each life event, consider how you felt during the event. Place an x in the columns that best reflect the key drivers for you at the time.

3   Add up the x's in each column and enter the total in the total row at the bottom of the worksheet.

4   Circle the Spiritual Milestone column heading that has the highest total. Are there other column totals within a few points of the highest total?
    If not, you have found your milestone!
    If there are other column totals within a few points of the highest total, re-look at your worksheet and for any experience with more than three factors and keep the top two key drivers..

5   Assess

   a.   What was your *first* reaction to your Spiritual Milestone?

| | |
|---|---|
| I'm surprised | |
| This makes sense | |
| This seems wrong | |
| Other | |

   b.   Which of these emotions describes your first reaction to your milestone?

| | | | |
|---|---|---|---|
| enthusiastic | defensive | hopeful | unsure | other |
| sad | positive | panic | resolute | |
| happy | anger | encouraged | shame | |

   c.   Does this Spiritual Milestone "feel right" to you? Why or why not?

   d.   Does your Spiritual Milestone feel relevant in your life now? If not, when did it cease to be? If yes, in what ways?

6   Complete the Vulnerability, Blocked Heart, and Awareness of Incapacity Triggers worksheets using the same difficult life events you listed in the Spiritual Milestone worksheet.

7   Fill in the blanks

   Vulnerability

   Blocked Heart

   Spiritual Millestone

   Awareness of Incapacity Trigger

8   Complete the following sentence, using your input from above:

   "During difficult situations today, because I feel _____ (insert your vulnerability), I (insert blocked heart) and find myself (insert Spiritual Milestone), causing (insert Awareness of Incapacity Trigger).

   "During difficult situations today, because I feel _____, I _____ and find myself _____ causing _____.

## Spiritual Milestone Worksheet

...select 1-3 feelings for each event

| | List difficult life events | How did you feel? | | | | | | | | | | | | | |
|---|---|---|---|---|---|---|---|---|---|---|---|---|---|---|---|
| | | Lacking | Separate | Sad | Guarded | Victimized | Chaotic | Regretful | Ashamed | Defensive | Yearning | Criticized | Angry |
| 1 | | | | | | | | | | | | | |
| 2 | | | | | | | | | | | | | |
| 3 | | | | | | | | | | | | | |
| 4 | | | | | | | | | | | | | |
| 5 | | | | | | | | | | | | | |
| 6 | | | | | | | | | | | | | |
| 7 | | | | | | | | | | | | | |
| 8 | | | | | | | | | | | | | |
| 9 | | | | | | | | | | | | | |
| 10 | | | | | | | | | | | | | |
| 11 | | | | | | | | | | | | | |
| 12 | | | | | | | | | | | | | |
| 13 | | | | | | | | | | | | | |
| 14 | | | | | | | | | | | | | |
| 15 | | | | | | | | | | | | | |
| | Total (circle highest score) | | | | | | | | | | | | |

Figure 3

Once your list of events is complete, pick one and spend a few moments recalling that event. Review it and evaluate whether each of the factors listed in the spreadsheet was a *key* part of how you felt at the time. If it was, place an x in that square. Several feelings may be applicable, but as a rule of thumb, I suggest you x only a few (one to three) for each event. Think about which feelings really *drove* that being a significant event in your life rather than how you felt as the event unfolded. The other feelings may be more of an outcome or something you saw in retrospect than a driving factor at the time. If you have any particular thoughts that arise during this review, jot them down. Take your time and note any emotions that may surface.

When complete, total the number of x's in each "How did you feel?" column. Typically, one feeling stands out among the crowd of twelve and that is your Spiritual Milestone. If you find you have more than one that are clustered at the highest total, you may want to go back and re-look at each event and perhaps limit yourself to fewer feelings for each event. That doesn't mean the other feelings weren't applicable, it simply helps to emphasize the biggest factors in determining your Spiritual Milestone. Another approach here is to add a few more difficult life events to your list and assess them to see if that makes your milestone clearer. There is, however, only *one* Spiritual Milestone.

Put a big circle around your Spiritual Milestone. While the experience is fresh, answer the questions on the worksheet and any others that come to mind for you.

If you're feeling like the DIY method isn't working for you today, give it another try another day. Alternatively, there are other ways to access your milestone, such as through prayer or meditation or asking your guides for help. Energy practitioners with this experience may also be of help to you.

## Once you've identified your Spiritual Milestone

When I first determined my Spiritual Milestone was yearning, I was initially very surprised. I simply didn't expect it. It then quickly resonated very deeply within me. It's like I felt it washing over me. I felt great compassion for myself, and I looked for what was connected to it. There was a lot connected to it.

Your reaction to your milestone may be different than mine. My guides tell me that about eight percent of people immediately embrace their Spiritual Milestone. Another twenty-two percent immediately reject theirs. The vast majority (seventy percent) of people are surprised by their Spiritual Milestone. That was me! I find it so interesting that such a vital piece of personal insight was not apparent to me. I now think of the Spiritual Milestone as a hidden pattern, and a very important one because it can hinder self-love. Understanding it, therefore, is a key step toward restoring that self-love.

You may somewhat identify with your Spiritual Milestone but have your doubts. Perhaps it was different than what you thought it would be. Let's be honest: none of these Spiritual Milestones is something we want. Chaotic? Shamed? Angry? No, thank you. When we *do* have awareness of our Spiritual Milestone, we often hide it, justify it, or pretend we have it under control. Regardless of how you are feeling about your Spiritual Milestone, I encourage you to read on and use some of the ideas below to perhaps relate more strongly in a way that is useful to you.

Why? What I came to learn from my guides is just how integrated and important the Spiritual Milestone is for all of us. *Every single one* of our sixteen Life Lessons is linked to our Spiritual Milestone in some way. We can only make so much progress until that milestone is resolved. That said, that's the way things are set up. That's the way it's designed and that's the way it works. The beauty of it is that knowing your Spiritual Milestone helps you understand it, and understanding it better can help you make progress on your path and shift into spiritual harmony.

We each have the opportunity to complete our Spiritual Milestone in this lifetime. How does that happen? The Spiritual Milestone is complete when our human consciousness expands to align with our essence. Our essence is a Divine bond of creativity and transfiguration. It is also our individual expression of pure consciousness and our benevolent access to genius. It is holy. It's when my consciousness of my Spiritual Milestone of yearning aligns with the pure consciousness of my essence. Pure consciousness is Divine consciousness. This means for me, my yearning becomes a lot *less* like my mortal-self yearning and a lot *more* like the Divine, which doesn't yearn.

The road to completion of the Spiritual Milestone is when we in a heartfelt way do the following:

- Recognize it
- Ask for help from the Divine
- Surrender it to the Divine
- Look at things as the Divine would look at them

For some of us, we may resist recognizing the Spiritual Milestone and stop right there. If my response to my Spiritual Milestone of yearning was "I do *not* yearn!", you would not be reading this book. For others, asking for help from the Divine or surrendering it to the Divine is a show-stopper. This can be a real challenge for those independent types among us who do *not* want help. If you do choose to take those important heartfelt steps and move forward beyond them, the next challenge is a big one. This is where we do our best to look at things as the Divine would look at them. This requires a shift and eventually begins to shift your life. Your guides will be right there with you the entire way if you ask them to be.

So what can you do now that you know your milestone? How can you move toward integrating it with understanding in your life? First, recognize that your Personal Framework and Life Lessons are designed to make your Spiritual Milestone an integral part of your life experience. You don't need to name your Spiritual Milestone in order to complete it. That said, knowing it may help you move more directly through the experiences you need to complete it.

Here are the top eleven things I recommend to consciously move along the path toward making your Spiritual Milestone complete:

1. **Remember it:** If your response to your milestone is "Oh, that's interesting" and to file it away in your drawer, your pathway to Spiritual Milestone completion will likely stay as it is now. Maybe you're okay with that. If you would prefer to consciously engage with it and change the trajectory of that path, keep some sort of visible reminder of it: post-it note on your laptop, screen-saver on your phone, etc. Consciously focus on it often.

2. **Notice it:** Start taking mental note when you find yourself in a day-to-day difficult life situation and think consciously about how your Spiritual Milestone may be connected to it. You might make a habit of thinking, "Oh, that's interesting. There it is again." Even

without doing something else differently, your understanding will broaden and your path will begin to shift.

3. **Ponder it:** When you notice your Spiritual Milestone cropping up in a way that doesn't serve you, give it some quality thought time or journal what happened and how your Spiritual Milestone is playing out. I'm not suggesting you do this every time, but try it with a few that seem meaningful to you. Consider other options of addressing it that aren't centered on your milestone. For instance, with my milestone of yearning, I often try to control things and end up thinking about it incessantly, which is not helpful. A non-yearning option may be to do the opposite by simply stopping my thought process around it. Easier said than done! Another option would be to simply not respond immediately and give it a day or two before re-engaging. Again, you may or may not follow-up, but simply recognizing there *are* other options will help you shift in a way that is helpful to you.

4. **Share it:** If you feel intrigued by what you've done so far, share your milestone and what you're learning with a good friend or someone else close to you that you trust and feel safe with. They may offer confirmation and ideas you haven't considered that help you along your path. Remember, we *all* have a Spiritual Milestone, so you sharing yours may also help others.

5. **Give yourself a pep talk:** Think of this as half time of the game of life. Maybe you're tired. Perhaps you're feeling the need to regroup. What you have *now* that you didn't have during the first half is insight into the Spiritual Milestone as a life theme. That's powerful information. Take a deep breath, remind yourself how important this work and your life is, and get back in the game!

6. **Ask your Guides:** If you have a great ongoing relationship with your guides, get their help with your Spiritual Milestone. They will be thrilled to help you. If you don't have a relationship with your guides, or you have an "I only talk to my guides on really special occasions" type of relationship with them, consider this an opportunity to get started working more with them. Re-read Chapter 2 on how to initiate the conversation. It's never too late to start consciously using this amazing Divinely-given resource. As a colleague once told me, "The second best time is now." We simply cannot complete the Spiritual Milestone without Divine help.

7. **Integrate it:** Spend some quality time meditating, praying, journaling, or otherwise reflecting on how and where in your life your Spiritual Milestone shows up. Ask for help from your guides and the Divine to make progress on it. Surrender it to the Divine.

8. **Forgive yourself:** We can be awfully hard on ourselves when it comes to things we perceive as a weakness or something that we think we need to fix. Remember, this Spiritual Milestone is not that! It is a vehicle to learn with and through that moves you forward. This is a good time to forgive the past, take a deep breath, and engage with it differently.

9. **Be grateful:** I know being grateful for such an ever-present challenge can be difficult, but it is not simply a hurdle to overcome. It is a means to a powerful end: growth of the level of the spirit. The good news is the benefits that come along with completing the Spiritual Milestone in this lifetime. I suggest you focus on those:

   • alleviate suffering
   • joyful progress along your life journey with self-love
   • inspire creativity
   • venture toward the Divine

10. **Set your intention:** Enlist the help of the universe! Remember, "the universe cooperates with a made-up mind." If it is your intention to make progress on your Spiritual Milestone, commit to that and "put it out there" to your team and to the universe. Put some energy and *umph* behind it. There is great power in sustained intention.

11. **Smile:** Now that you've made-up your mind, let it happen. Smile. Live your life with intention and happiness.

## More DIY

Since you invested a bit of your heart in soul in this list of difficult life events, let's put it to some more good use! The pivotal Turn of Fortune included several steps that were related to the initiation of the Spiritual Milestone. Let's use it to learn more.

## Vulnerability

In the Turn of Fortune, preceding the misfortune was a vulnerability that occurred sometime in the year prior. That same vulnerability may still be at play today. My guides tell me there are seven pre-Turn of Fortune vulnerabilities. These vulnerabilities cause us to feel unsafe or "less than" in some way that simply was not there before, thus its importance to us as young children when it happens. These vulnerabilities are:

- minimized
- criticized
- anguished
- isolated
- anxious
- longing
- conflicted

Using the same list of difficult life events from Figure 3, assess if any of these vulnerabilities were relevant to each experience. For each event, please select one or two vulnerabilities from the Vulnerability Worksheet (Figure 4, page 89), ideally the first that comes to mind, and put an x in that column. When complete, add up the x's in each column. The highest score is the vulnerability that accompanies your Spiritual Milestone. If you have two of them that are very close and distinctly different in quantity than the others, they both may apply. For me, my vulnerability was anxious regarding another separation from my family due to a different medical concern.

## Blocked Heart

The blocked heart was an emotional response in the Turn of Fortune that resulted in certain characteristics or shields that stay with us well beyond the event and may show up in times of great difficulty. It is helpful to know what that characteristic is and if it is not serving you, to address it through a means that you choose. This could include awareness, meditation, prayer, or energy work. The six characteristics or shields are:

- Back Away
- Resist
- Think Twice
- Cut Things Off
- Cover Up
- Keep Mum

Using the same list of difficult life events, assess if any of these characteristics were relevant to each experience. Please select only one characteristic from the Blocked Heart Worksheet (Figure 5, page 90) ideally the first that comes to mind, and put an x in that column. When complete, add up the x's in each column. The highest score is the characteristic that accompanies your Spiritual Milestone. For me, my blocked heart characteristic is "resist."

## Awareness of Incapacity Triggers

In the Turn of Fortune, after the misfortune there is a trigger that results in an awareness of incapacity, which then leads to a sense of disillusionment in the life journey. An awareness of incapacity in this context is the realization that we simply understand we cannot do something we thought we could. The four situations below are the precursor or trigger to this awareness of incapacity:

- fear
- pain
- abuse
- humiliation

Using the same list of difficult life events, assess if any of these triggers were relevant to each experience. Please select only one trigger from the Awareness of Incapacities Worksheet (Figure 6, page 91), ideally the first that comes to mind, and put an x in that column. When complete, add up the x's in each column. The highest score is the awareness of incapacity trigger from your Turn of Fortune. For me, my trigger was fear about losing my mom.

## Vulnerability Worksheet

...select 1-2 feelings for each event

| Copy difficult life events from Spiritual Milestone worksheet | How did you feel? | | | | | | | |
|---|---|---|---|---|---|---|---|---|
| | Minimized | Criticized | Anguished | Isolated | Anxious | Longing | Conflicted |
| 1 | | | | | | | |
| 2 | | | | | | | |
| 3 | | | | | | | |
| 4 | | | | | | | |
| 5 | | | | | | | |
| 6 | | | | | | | |
| 7 | | | | | | | |
| 8 | | | | | | | |
| 9 | | | | | | | |
| 10 | | | | | | | |
| 11 | | | | | | | |
| 12 | | | | | | | |
| 13 | | | | | | | |
| 14 | | | | | | | |
| 15 | | | | | | | |
| Total (circle highest scoring factor) | | | | | | | |

Figure 4

## Blocked Heart Worksheet

...select one action for each event

| | Copy difficult life events from Spiritual Milestone worksheet | What did you do? | | | | | |
|---|---|---|---|---|---|---|---|
| | | Back Away | Resist | Think Twice | Cut Things Off | Cover Up | Keep Mum |
| 1 | | | | | | | |
| 2 | | | | | | | |
| 3 | | | | | | | |
| 4 | | | | | | | |
| 5 | | | | | | | |
| 6 | | | | | | | |
| 7 | | | | | | | |
| 8 | | | | | | | |
| 9 | | | | | | | |
| 10 | | | | | | | |
| 11 | | | | | | | |
| 12 | | | | | | | |
| 13 | | | | | | | |
| 14 | | | | | | | |
| 15 | | | | | | | |
| Total (circle highest scoring action) | | | | | | | |

Figure 5

## Awareness of Incapacity Triggers Worksheet

...selecte one feeling for each event

| | Copy difficult life events from Spiritual Milestone worksheet | What did you feel? | | | |
| --- | --- | --- | --- | --- | --- |
| | | Fear | Pain | Abuse | Humiliation |
| 1 | | | | | |
| 2 | | | | | |
| 3 | | | | | |
| 4 | | | | | |
| 5 | | | | | |
| 6 | | | | | |
| 7 | | | | | |
| 8 | | | | | |
| 9 | | | | | |
| 10 | | | | | |
| 11 | | | | | |
| 12 | | | | | |
| 13 | | | | | |
| 14 | | | | | |
| 15 | | | | | |
| | Total (circle highest scoring factor) | | | | |

Figure 6

## How Do They All Fit Together?

You now have four pieces of information that generally dominated in your list of difficult life experiences. Please list them as indicated:

Vulnerability: _____

Blocked Heart: _____

Spiritual Milestone: _____

Awareness of Incapacity Trigger: _____

Now use them to complete this sentence and gain insight into how these Turn of Fortune factors may be playing out for you now in difficult situations:

> "Because I feel (insert vulnerability), I (insert blocked heart) and find myself (insert Spiritual Milestone) concerning that which seems unattainable, causing (insert awareness of incapacity trigger)."

For example, using my worksheets:

> Vulnerability: anxious
> Blocked Heart: resist
> Spiritual Milestone: yearning
> Awareness of Incapacity: fear

For Sally: "Because I feel anxious, I resist and find myself yearning concerning that which seems unattainable, causing fear."

This insight describes the way I act today, sixty years after the original Turn of Fortune in times of distress or great difficulty. As I reflected on this, I could see it clearly. I then considered the same statement regarding my chronic weight issue: it felt very relevant to my weight issue and the "behind the scenes" dynamic that goes on within me. As I applied my Attracting Joy method to this sentence, it was very low-vibration and the realms of human motivation and obsession were at play. I addressed it using the method and began to dig deeper.

I found a few other chronic areas that also seemed relevant to this approach and worked on them using Attracting Joy. I asked my guides if the issues I experience today that stem from the Turn of Fortune had a name and was told it was an agreement based in a self-limiting belief. I use the word "agreement" here as author Don Miguel Ruiz explained in his book *The Four Agreements*, where he describes them as the "source of self-limiting beliefs that rob us of joy and create needless suffering."

I certainly feel that was the case with my three issues. I asked how many agreements to self-limiting beliefs people generally have and was told the answer is five to nine, with an average of six. I was also told the agreements to self-limiting beliefs can begin to form after the Turn of Fortune and on average last about sixty-six years. These do not originate in the Personal Framework when we come into this life—rather, we create them in our Personal Framework during our lifetime.

We may attribute our challenges in life to what we are feeling and doing right now. Often, though, they have their roots much deeper into our life experience than we realize. The Turn of Fortune holds the answer to many of the chronic struggles we endure.

## Reflective Questions to Consider

1. Was it uncomfortable to reflect on a particularly difficult life event in the life review? What about it still triggers you?
2. Is asking the Divine for help with your Spiritual Milestone and surrendering it to the Divine difficult or easy for you to do? Why is that?

# 13

## Attracting Joy

Today is another opportunity to look within and allow something remarkable to happen. We have within us capabilities unrealized and unimagined. If we only knew what is waiting to be brought forth through us, we may stop everything we are doing and focus there.

We are a miraculous expression of the Divine. There is a field of loving possibility that surrounds us at all times. We are distracted by other attractor fields that make it very difficult to notice that which the Divine has offered to us with grace and benevolence. It remains available to us, ready to offer its gifts of creativity and transfiguration. We only need to ask.

I was reading a book a when it happened for me. I was working on my weight issue and looking for insights, opening myself up for a solution beyond what I had been working on and with for several years. I felt a shift where suddenly words and phrases seemed to jump off the pages. It was like I was being gifted information that I needed. To my surprise, I knew right away that I would use this to develop an energy method. Developing an energy method was not something I ever considered doing, but at that moment, it felt necessary and inevitable. I was excited and energized to dig in.

What unfolded over the next few years of working daily on this calling was a gift of discovery. Every day something new came to the fore. The method would expand like an accordion over weeks or months and then collapse overnight down to a few simple truths. Each time that happened, it seemed to propel me forward with a new set of things to explore and expand upon. That too, would then coalesce into something simple and profound to build upon again. And so the process continued. Many times along the way I asked my guides, "Is this it?" I don't ask that anymore. I expect Attracting Joy will continue to unfold as my consciousness continues to expand.

The Attracting Joy method differs from other energy methodologies I have worked with as a practitioner and client. I see two distinct differences.

The first difference is approaching desires from the standpoint of the integrated spirit, essence, and mortal self. This approach developed over time, beginning with looking at the spirit and the mortal self individually. It later evolved to include all three aspects as a unified whole when addressing any issue or goal. This approach has been helpful in sustaining the results clients are seeking.

The second difference has to do with using the Personal Framework as the realm of addressing the issues. This allows us to tie directly back to the Divine design for our life.

Attracting Joy meets the client where they are with their day-to-day and long-term concerns about a sense of loss, pain, or yearning they are experiencing in their life and wraps it in the light of Divine wholeness. It is illuminated in that oneness to support their desire and the courage to change to make the path easier. This inspires awareness of the client on many levels to attract the joy they seek. We are intended to live our lives knowing there is another realm of possibilities available to guide us toward true joy and our infinite self.

Clients come to me for lots of reasons, each of them intensely personal. The issue may be chronic physical, emotional, or mental pain that continues despite their many efforts within the traditional medical community or via other alternative methods. Sometimes, like with me, there is a yearning that drives them. Other clients may feel stuck in some way, like when a career or relationship feels stale. Many times they are reaching for a goal of some sort.

If you're new to energy work, here are a few things that may be helpful to understand:

1. Practitioners may access the information they need to help you in different ways. With Attracting Joy, I use "muscle testing" or

kinesiology to remotely get the answers to questions I ask your heart and your unconscious mind on your behalf. I won't go into that method specifically here, but there is a lot of information available online to those interested in learning more.

2. Energy work in and of itself does not heal a person. I do not consider myself an energy healer, but rather a person who works with the energy that limits your body's natural ability to heal itself. I help people transform the energies interfering with their body's profound healing. The client does the healing.

3. Many forms of energy work are done remotely. For Attracting Joy, you do not need to physically be in the same location as the practitioner. Energy works with the principle of non-locality. This was particularly beneficial during the isolation of the pandemic, but is equally helpful in connecting with practitioners that may be far from your location.

4. Some people are wary of energy work, fearing it may be contrary to their view of the Divine. I find this interesting because for me, this journey into spirituality has brought me closer to the Divine, much closer than I could have ever dreamed. That said, I certainly respect people's choices to get help in a way that is consistent with their belief system.

The benefits of working energetically on issues that matter to you can be significant for those who seek it. In whatever path you choose to help you with your issues, I wish you good health, abundance, and love.

## Reflective Questions to Consider

1. Have you ever considered working with an energy practitioner? This is a great question to explore with your guides.
2. Interested in learning more? Go to sallyheidtke.com

# 14

# Living with Understanding

It may seem as if we are struggling aimlessly, but there is a Divine order beneath the radar of our understanding. It is a purposeful, intended movement toward the Divine that makes each choice a step that moves us closer to being infinite on this non-linear path.

We are Divine. We are infinite. We all exist in a system of infinite possibility that we access through our Personal Framework. We are an important part of that system in these mortal bodies we occupy. Our contribution to the "all that is" comes through fully experiencing this life on Earth. As we try to make sense of the mysteries in our lives, we can look to our guides for help. They are our infinite connection to the Divine and our infinite self.

The structures outlined in this book provide a means to understand and approach our chronic challenges. Our struggles can lead us to improved capability. Although at times we may feel helpless and hopeless, Divine support is always available to encourage us.

Allowing the love of the Divine to pull us through the trauma and everyday challenges that life brings is a source of stability that sustains us. We can rise above our Spiritual Milestone and its patterns to shift into spiritual harmony. As we become infinite, our love magnifies in ways and forms beyond our comprehension. This love confirms our Divine alignment and creates new potential. The broadening of our love supports the expansion of others to do the same. The Divine awaits you with grace that transcends time.

May your love light the world.

# Acknowledgements

I have always viewed each decade of my life as more interesting and satisfying than the last. So many of the experiences from my past came together somewhere in the process of writing this book. A few of them made it to the page, but I am grateful for them all and what they taught me. Experiences are simply an expression of the people you meet along the way. I am thankful for each of you.

So often the Universe constructs events that take us exactly where we need to be and who we need to be with. I am so thankful that guidance brought me to the desk of my editor, Kathryn Chandika Liedel, whose direction, input, questions, and enthusiasm were exactly what I needed.

I feel blessed with the widespread support I have had in writing this book. I am especially grateful to Cassandra Greer, Beth Provencher, LouAnne Koerschner, and Paula Allen for their help through the final editing process.

I am deeply grateful to my guide team for their unwavering and patient support of me in all aspects of my life, including this book. I look forward to where we go next!

I am filled with love for my family and their unwavering encouragement, support, and love. You all mean the world to me!

This book was written with the loving support and encouragement of my husband Dean, who somehow knew how to support me without me even knowing how to ask for the support I needed. Thank you for believing in me.

# About Sally Heidtke-Intuitive

Sally Heidtke welcomed her intuitive self into her life about eight years ago. She continues to explore that relationship to better love and understand the Divine's will for her and her greatest and highest good. Sally Heidtke's life and her intuitive practice expanded significantly with the development of the Attracting Joy method, which continues to evolve. She works with clients from around the world to assist them in their healing process and in attaining life goals.

Learn more at sallyheidtke.com

PGIL2023USA